YOU DON'T NEED AN ACCOUNTANT

About the Author

Ray Fitzgerald is a Chartered Accountant. He is chief executive of Ray Fitzgerald Financial Training and has spent much of his working life teaching non-accounting managers the effects their decisions have on the financial health of their businesses. He has written three previous books and has also written a module of the IOD Diploma in Company Direction. All of his publications have received superb reviews.

You Don't Need An Accountant

RAY FITZGERALD

BLACKHALL
Publishing

This book was typeset by
Gough Typesetting Services for
BLACKHALL PUBLISHING
26 Eustace Street
Dublin 2
Ireland

e-mail: blackhall@tinet.ie

ISBN: 1 901657 81 7

A catalogue record for this book is available
from the British Library.

Printed in Ireland by
Colourbooks Ltd

PREFACE

Throughout my working life I have devoted much of my time to teaching non-accountants the aspects of finance that they must understand and apply if they are to maintain a healthy business. I have done this by explaining the jargon and concepts of finance in simple English. My students are always business people. Some of them start by being terrified of finance; most of them are pleasantly surprised when they discover that they are the real financial controllers in their businesses and must participate in making and implementing financial policy.

You are the proprietor of a small firm. Your top priority should be your health. Another important priority is the health of your business. In large companies, the financial controller is the corporate doctor. Smaller companies cannot usually afford the cost of an in-house accountant. In such circumstances the chief executive must take the responsibility for financial health. To do this effectively you must be able to interpret financial statements correctly and to diagnose the financial consequences of your business decisions.

As you read this book you will be pleased to discover that there are only about a dozen issues that can seriously damage the financial health of your business. You will learn how to recognise these issues and how to manage them correctly. This will turn you into an effective financial controller and explain why I have called the book *You Don't Need An Accountant*.

I have tried to make the book enjoyable as well as interesting. This is a hard task with a 'dry' topic, such as finance. I hope you will find the presentation style attractive and relevant to your need to become a capable part-time financial controller.

Books on business and finance are bedevilled by the fact that accounting rules and taxation rates vary from country to country. In writing this book, I decided to use the accounting laws relating to the UK and Ireland and tax laws related to the UK. This decision should not affect the potential of readers from other jurisdictions to benefit greatly from reading and applying its contents.

Ray Fitzgerald
April 1999

CONTENTS

CHAPTER 1

UNDERSTANDING FINANCIAL STATEMENTS: THE GENERAL MEDICAL

Prudent people occasionally visit a doctor for a general check-up even though they have no symptoms of medical problems. In the same way financial statements provide the basis for checking the health of a business. There are three major statements:

- the profit and loss account;
- the balance sheet;
- the cash flow statement.

These statements are like the major tools of a doctor. The profit and loss account is the pulse test. It measures the rate of growth or decline in sales costs and profits. The balance sheet is the thermometer. It tests financial stability. A high temperature occurs when a business has too much debt. The cash flow statement is the blood pressure. If the heart of the business is not pumping enough cash the business can die.

Business law requires that these statements be prepared each financial year. The wise business will require them to be produced more often. Cash generation, financial stability and profitability need to be monitored regularly. Operating conditions can change so rapidly that only a foolish board of directors would wait a full year for the preparation and review of financial statements. The board and management of a business must be able to interpret these financial reports correctly. To do this, they need to understand the purposes of such statements and the accounting policies and conventions that are used therein. The preparation and interpretation of accounts should be a regular item on the board agenda.

The first step in an effective control process is to prepare budgeted financial statements that will sketch the route to acceptable and attainable performance. As the financial year unfolds the actual results must be computed and compared with the budget. Where actual performance fails to at least equal the budget, actions must be taken to overcome shortfall(s).

I have no doubt that your business needs financial statements to be prepared at least once in each quarter. The only matter that you need to consider is who to get to prepare them promptly and accurately. Many owners ask their auditors to prepare the statements. The trouble with this is that, even for a small and uncomplicated business, it is likely to cost at least £5,000 per year. This is a heavy cost for a small firm. Sometimes it may prove cheaper to equip the bookkeeper or chief executive with the skills required to prepare the statements. No matter who prepares your financial reports you will need the skills to interpret them correctly. You must be able to search within the figures for strengths and weaknesses. Key relationships, called ratios, provide the basis for identifying things that need to be addressed.

In this chapter, I will examine the purposes of financial statements, the accounting principles contained in them and help you to understand them. In Chapter 2, I will show you how to analyse them correctly. The rest of the book will pinpoint the financial aspect of your business decisions. It will explain how these decisions will help or hinder profitability and financial stability. These are the cornerstones of survival and success in business.

Figures 1.1–1.3: Skeleton Financial Statements

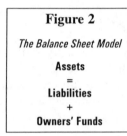

Figure 1	Figure 2	Figure 3
The Profit and Loss Model	*The Balance Sheet Model*	*The Cash Flow Model*
Sales	Assets	Cash Inflows
–	=	–
Costs	Liabilities	Cash Outflows
=	+	=
Profit or Loss	Owners' Funds	Change in Cash

UNDERSTANDING THE PROFIT AND LOSS ACCOUNT

There is a popular misconception that, provided you end each month with more cash in the bank, or a lower overdraft, than you started with, your business has performed satisfactorily. While improved liquidity is a valuable indicator of performance it does not reveal whether a profit or a loss has been incurred. Nor does it reveal whether the business is better or worse equipped to face its future. The profit and loss account is the most important indicator of business performance, albeit not the only one. It goes far beyond the confines of cash inflows and outflows to measure operating results. It is a document that is of major importance to your directors, staff and shareholders.

In principle, measuring the profit or loss is a straightforward task. The skeleton in Figure 1.1 shows that sales minus costs equals profit, unless the costs exceed the sales in which case a loss results. In practice it is not as easy as it sounds.

The first problem is with the word 'sales'. It means the value of goods or services supplied to customers, whether they have been paid for or not. The sales value is shown net of Value Added Tax (VAT). This is because you are simply acting as a tax collector for the tax authorities. You will have to make your profit out of the sales net of VAT. Even when a credit sale proves uncollectable it is recorded as a sale. The bad debt will be deducted as a cost. This corrects for what has turned out to be an ill-advised sale. Note that, if sales are growing and the business is selling on credit, the sales are likely to be greater than the collections from customers. This is the principal reason why a profit and loss account provides a poor indicator of liquidity.

The second problem is that the cost of sales has to be measured and charged against the sales. Consider the following example: Anne Sharp recently started in business. She bought 1,000 laptop computers at £235 each. The invoice specified a charge of £200 per laptop plus Value Added Tax of £35 leading to a total charge of £235,000. In her first month of trading Anne sold 800 laptops at £352.50 each. Invoices to her customers specified a charge of £300 plus VAT of £52.50. To simplify the profit and loss account we will assume that Anne had no other costs. At the end of the month Anne wants to know whether she made a profit or a loss and how much. Take out a blank sheet of paper, a pen and a calculator and try to help her before reading on.

You may think the answer is £47,000 or £40,000. Both of these answers are almost certainly wrong. Before preparing the accounts, Anne will have to count and value her stock. In preparing the valuation of stock, I advise Anne that the financial reporting standard for small enterprises (FRSSE) requires that stock must be valued at the lower of cost and net realisable value. For present purposes you can assume that net realisable value caters for items that have been damaged and may not realise what they cost. Anne counted her stock and reported that she had 200 laptops all in excellent condition. Based on this information the profit and loss account might be reported as in Table 1.1.

Table 1.1: Profit and Loss Account

	Incorrect 1	Incorrect 2	Correct
Sales	282,000	240,000	240,000
Cost of sales	235,000	200,000	160,000
Profit	47,000	40,000	80,000

Why is the first version incorrect? Because the sales and cost of sales include VAT. Anne was charged £35,000 of VAT by her supplier. She will recover this by deducting it from the £42,000 that she charged her customers. She will pay the tax authorities the difference of £7,000. Why is the second version incorrect? It fails to recognise the value to Anne of the 200 laptops not yet sold. Following the rule in the FRSSE they are worth £40,000 to her. This is 200 at £200 each net of VAT. Anne should compute her cost of sales as follows.

Purchases	200,000
Less closing stock	40,000
Cost of sales	160,000

Using this figure we arrive at the correct profit of £80,000. You may want to kick yourself if you did not get the right answer. Logic should have told you that if she sold 800 laptops and made a profit of £100 on each one her total profit should be £80,000. It is important to note that if one laptop had been scrapped or stolen Anne's profit would be reduced to £79,800.

To ensure that you really understand the previous example we will prepare the profit and loss account for Anne's second month in business. She bought 600 laptops at £235 each and sold 700 laptops at £352.50 each. Both figures include VAT at 17.5 per cent. Did she make a profit or loss and how much? Return to your blank sheet of paper and try to work it out before reading on.

The logical answer is that if no laptops have been scrapped or stolen Anne should have earned a profit of £70,000. Her profit and loss account will verify this as follows.

Sales		210,000
Opening stock	40,000	
Purchases	120,000	
Cost of goods available for sale	160,000	
Closing stock	20,000	
Cost of sales		140,000
Profit		70,000

By deducting the 200 unsold computers, in computing the cost of sales for month one, Anne deferred the cost until they were sold. That is why they were brought back into account in month two. Anne had 800 laptops available for sale and these cost £160,000. What would have been the profit in month two if five laptops had been stolen? The answer is £69,000. The accounts would show this as follows.

Sales		210,000
Opening stock	40,000	
Purchases	120,000	
Cost of goods available for sale	160,000	
Closing stock	19,000	
Cost of sales		141,000
Profit		69,000

Calculation of the cost of sales is quite difficult in more complicated businesses such as manufacturing and construction. The problem is that these businesses add value to the materials purchased. Instead of reporting purchases these businesses will have to calculate the cost of production. For example, costs, such as factory rent and rates, will have to be included in the cost of production as well as purchases of materials and payments to production staff. The problem is further exacerbated because such organisations normally hold three kinds of stocks:

(a) raw materials;

(b) work in progress;

(c) finished goods.

An illustration of the problems involved is presented in Appendix 1 on page 22. If your business is wholesaling, retailing or a service industry the appendix may be of little relevance to you and you may ignore it.

The third problem associated with profit and loss accounts is that the report is of costs related to the period even if they were paid for in a previous or subsequent accounting period. For example, you will normally be charged for your January consumption of electricity in February. Nevertheless, this charge should be included in the January profit and loss account. This is done by making an accrual. The amount may have to be estimated if the bill has not been received when the January profit and loss account is being prepared. In the December profit and loss account you should have accrued for the bill paid in January. For example, Bertie Bright had made an accrual of £278 for electricity used in December. In January his actual bill for December came to £285.43. He decided that his bill for January would come to £300 and reported his cost for January as £307.43. This was made up of an under provision of £7.43 for December plus the accrued estimate for January. For those interested in bookkeeping the ledger account will resemble Table 1.2.

Table 1.2: Electricity Account

To cash	285.43	By accrual brought down	278.00
To accrual carried down	300.00	By profit and loss	307.43
	585.43		585.43

The accrual is a debt due by the business. It must also be reported as a liability in the balance sheet, as we will see later in this chapter.

An example of a cost that has been paid in advance is fire insurance. Last July, Bertie Bright paid his fire insurance account of £4,800 covering him for the year that will end on 30 June next. In his January accounts Bertie will report a charge of £400. In spite of the fact that nothing was paid in January, his fire insurance certainly cost him £400 for the month. For those interested in bookkeeping the ledger account will resemble Table 1.3.

Table 1.3: Fire Insurance Account

To prepayment	2,400	By prepayment	2,000
		By profit and loss	400
			2,400

The fourth important issue in preparing a profit and loss account is depreciation. Some expenditure, such as electricity, has no ongoing value. You simply pay for it as you use it. Other expenditure, such as the purchase of a company car, is quite different. Such expenditure has a substantial ongoing value. Later in this chapter we will see that things, such as cars, are included in the balance sheet as an asset. They also have a significant impact on the profit and loss account.

Consider *Driver Ltd.* On its first day in business, the company bought a car for £20,000. At the end of the year they had experienced a loss of value through using the car in the business. This loss of value had to be reflected in the profit and loss account. How should the loss be calculated? One approach might be to assess the market value. Deducting this from the cost would identify the loss of value. Suppose that a car dealer offered a trade-in value of £14,000. The loss of value could be said to be £6,000. The trade-in value is not usually a satisfactory way of measuring the loss. Driver Ltd probably has no intention of selling the car. To assess the loss of value correctly Driver Ltd needs to answer two questions. Firstly, how long will the car be kept? Suppose the answer is three years. Secondly, what will Driver Ltd expect to get for the car when they sell it three years from now? Suppose the answer to this is £8,000. Combining these predictions we can conclude that the loss of value that will be experienced over the full life of the car is expected to be £12,000. The normal approach to estimating the depreciation is to divide this loss of value by the expected life of the car. This is called straight line depreciation and leads to an annual charge of £4,000. Equally, dividing the loss by the 36 month life leads to a monthly depreciation charge of £333. The depreciation charge will be included in the expenses in the profit and loss account. It will also be deducted from the value of the asset in the balance sheet. The relevant figures are as in Table 1.4.

Table 1.4: Depreciation Charge

	After 6 months	After 1 year	After 2 years	After 3 years
Cost	20,000	20,000	20,000	20,000
Charge for period	(2,000)	(4,000)	(4,000)	(4,000)
Previous charge	–	–	(4,000)	(8,000)
Book value	18,000	16,000	12,000	8,000

The book value will be shown in the balance sheet as we will see later. It represents what the car is worth to the business on a continuing use basis. I believe that such a valuation is more relevant than the market value. In each of the months that the car is used in the business, a depreciation charge of £333 will be made in the profit and loss account. The depreciation charge for three months will be £1,000 and for twelve months will be £4,000. Suppose that at the end of the third year the car is sold for £9,000. With the benefit of hindsight, the depreciation charge was slightly too high. By including a profit on sale of £1,000 in the profit and loss account the overcharge is corrected. Equally, if the car was sold for £7,500 the depreciation charge would have proved to be inadequate. Driver Ltd would correct this by reporting a loss on sale of £500 in the third year profit and loss account. Another company, that owned a similar car, might intend to keep it for five years. It might anticipate a trade-in value of £4,000. This company would use an annual depreciation charge of £3,200. The value of the car would then be shown in the balance sheet at the end of the first year at £16,800. The fact that these two businesses used slightly different assumptions does not make the reported value of their cars incorrect. It simply reflects different opinions of the ongoing value of the two cars.

When all of the costs, other than interest, have been charged against sales, the amount that is left is reported as the operating profit or loss. This figure will be of immense importance to the bankers. It provides the platform for the repayment of the interest and capital elements of any loans that the bank has made to a business. Interest is then deducted from the operating profit or added to the operating loss. The resultant figure is the profit or loss before tax.

The tax authorities regard the profit before tax as the most important figure in the accounts of a business. This provides the basis for their claim for corporation tax. The business will not have to pay the corporation tax bill for some time after the profit is disclosed. Nevertheless, a portion of the profit must be earmarked for future payment of this tax liability. This earmarking is called a provision. The corporation tax provision is deducted from the profit before tax. The resultant figure is the profit after tax.

Many shareholders regard the profit after tax as the most important figure in the accounts. It provides the platform upon which any dividends will be declared. Later in this book we will see that a wise company will not pay all of the profit after tax to shareholders as a dividend. Some of the profit will be retained to contribute towards the growth of the business. When the board decide how much of the profit to retain and how much to distribute as a dividend the profit and loss can be completed. This is done by deducting the proposed dividend from the profit after tax leaving the retained earnings, see Table 1.5.

Table 1.5: Example Profit and Loss Account: Bullet Proof Ltd

Last year		This year
324,997	Sales	448,501
212,873	Cost of sales [1]	307,223
112,124	Gross profit	141,278
72,590	Administration, selling and distribution	99,732
39,534	Operating profit	41,546
10,615	Interest paid	8,503
28,919	Profit before tax	33,043
8,714	Corporation tax	9,436
20,205	Profit after tax	23,607
5,000	Proposed dividend	6,500
15,205	Retained earnings	17,107

[1] **Cost of sales**

124,345	Purchases	176,249
42,186	Production labour	56,144
55,836	Other production costs	89,683
(9,494)	Increase in stocks	(14,853)
212,873	Cost of sales	307,223

[2] **Statutory information**

18,143	Depreciation	19,125
69,438	Staff remuneration	86,143
5	Staff numbers	6
1,864	Auditors' remuneration	1,854

Segmental analysis is not disclosed as, in the opinion of the directors, it would place the company at a competitive disadvantage.

Two major comments must be made about the summarised profit and loss account of Bullet Proof Ltd. Firstly, it provides too little information to be of use to management and the board of directors to assess business performance. The profit and loss account, to be discussed at management and board meetings, should provide a detailed breakdown of the costs. It should also compare the actual figures with the budget and identify variances that occurred. The skeleton profit and loss account is presented in a form that is used to report to the shareholders and for filing. Secondly, by law the notes to these accounts must include information on things such as the remuneration of directors and auditors. Information of this type is immensely important. It puts the reported profit or loss in context and provides information that will facilitate the shareholders' in the election of directors and auditors at the annual general meeting.

THE BALANCE SHEET

Unlike the profit and loss account, which provides a picture of business performance covering a period of time, the balance sheet paints a picture of a business at a moment in time. In the picture you will see:

(a) the things that a business owns (called assets);

(b) the sources of finance that the owners raised in order to enable them to own the assets.

These funds are of two major types:

(a) borrowings (called liabilities);

(b) shareholder investments.

The Assets in a Balance Sheet

Before reading on, take a blank sheet of paper and write down all the things that your business owns. I expect that your list includes things such as land, buildings, furniture, computers, cars and cash. If your business is manufacturing you will also have included plant and machinery. If your business is manufacturing or trading you will also have included stock in your list. One important asset that you may have omitted is money due from customers. These sales that have not yet been paid for are called trade debtors. They are a very important asset in the balance sheet of businesses that sell on credit. In the profit and loss account section of this chapter, we explained how fire insurance may be prepaid. Is the fact that you have paid for the fire insurance for the next six months of value to your business? Yes, it is. As such it must be recorded and reported as an asset. Another asset that is found in some balance sheets is the value of shares in other businesses. These are called investments. In the world of mergers, takeovers and international marketing, goodwill and brands are important assets. For example, the registered name Coca Cola is probably the best known and valuable brand in the world. In preparing a balance sheet the assets are divided into two major groups:

(a) fixed assets;

(b) current assets.

Fixed Assets

Fixed assets are items that are of ongoing value to the business. In the profit and loss account section we explored the valuation of a car by Driver Ltd There are many other types of fixed assets. Some examples include:

- plant and machinery in a manufacturing company;
- a stallion in a stud farm;
- Roy Keane in Manchester United;
- a hanger in an airport company;
- an office block;
- goodwill;
- brands;
- patents;
- investments in other businesses.

Some of these assets have very different characteristics. They are divided into three sub-groups:

(a) tangible fixed assets;

(b) intangible fixed assets;

(c) financial fixed assets.

The first five items in the bulleted list above are tangible fixed assets: you can touch them. The next three items are intangible: they provide a hope for future profitable sales. The final item, investments, is a financial fixed asset. The characteristics of investments are somewhat different from those of tangible or intangible fixed assets.

Current Assets

Unlike fixed assets, which tend to remain constant for long periods, current assets change from day to day. Major items found in current assets are:

(a) stocks;

(b) trade debtors;

(c) prepayments;

(d) cash.

For example stock changes every time a supplier delivers materials or a sale is made. Equally, prepayments decline with the passage of time. Cash is the most volatile asset.

Valuing the Assets

Item:	Valuation method.
Stock:	Count it and apply the supplier or manufactured cost.
Trade debtors:	Decide which debts are collectable.
Prepayments:	Reduce them in line with the passage of time.
Cash:	Count it.
Land:	Show it at cost. It should be revalued at least every five years. Tend to appreciate with the passage of time.
Buildings:	Show them at cost less depreciation. They should be revalued at least every five years. Tend to appreciate with the passage of time.
Other tangible:	Show them at cost less depreciation.
Intangible:	Examined in Appendix 2 on page 24.
Financial:	Examined in Appendix 2 on page 24.

Financing the Assets

As explained at the start of this section, the assets are funded through borrowings and owners' investment. The term 'balance sheet' is derived from the fact that the funds must exactly equal the assets. Borrowings may be for short or long periods of time. For accounting purposes short is defined as under one year.

Borrowings due and payable in under one year include:

• trade creditors (amounts due to suppliers);

• accruals (unbilled expenses);

• bank overdrafts;

• short-term bank loans (e.g. stocking loans in a car dealership);

• corporation tax (provision made in the profit and loss account);

- other unpaid taxes (e.g. PAYE and VAT);

- proposed dividends (provision made in the profit and loss account);

- the current portion of long-term bank borrowings. (For example, if a £100,000 bank loan has to be repaid in five equal annual instalments. The first instalment is due to be paid in six months' time, £20,000 must be included in short-term borrowings.)

The books should reveal the amount of each of these liabilities.

Loans that are due and payable in beyond one year are shown separately. The most frequent example is the long-term portion of a bank loan. In the example above £80,000 of the bank loan is due and payable in beyond one year.

HOW THE OWNERS PROVIDE FUNDS TO A BUSINESS

The owners provide funds in three ways. Firstly, they buy shares from the business. This is called the share capital. Note that buying shares from an existing holder does not provide funds to a business. Such a transaction has no effect on its share capital. Secondly, they provide funds by forgoing their right to withdraw all of the profits earned as dividends. As the sales of a business increase, the assets also tend to rise. If all of the growth in assets is financed by borrowings, the debts can become excessive. The retained earnings (often called a revenue reserve) help to ensure that the owners continue to make an adequate contribution towards the funding of the additional assets. Finally, they make a further contribution towards the assets of a business that is not always recognised. For example, a trading company bought its building six years ago for £85,000. In the most recent balance sheet the building was shown at £74,800 (2 per cent depreciation was deducted for each year). The chief executive asked an auctioneer to determine the current worth of the building. The valuer said it was worth £150,000. By holding this appreciating asset, the shareholders had on paper made a profit of £75,200. A wise board will include the £150,000 valuation in the balance sheet. To do so it must also recognise an increased shareholder investment. This additional investment is called a revaluation reserve. It amounts to £75,200 and balances the books. Failure to include the revised valuation might expose the business to the unwanted attention of an 'asset stripper'. It is good practice to revalue appreciating assets, such as land and buildings, at least once every five years. Note that in a property company the treatment would not be the same. Properties are the stock in trade of such businesses.

Table 1.6: Example Balance Sheet: Bullet Proof Ltd

Last year			This year
191,388	Tangible fixed assets [1]		187,263
	Current assets		
49,273	Stocks	64,126	
119,063	Debtors [4]	128,143	
15,895	Cash	19,145	
184,231		211,414	
	Amounts due and payable in		
(101,254)	under one year [2]	(127,205)	84,209
274,365	Net assets		271,472
	Financed by:		
100,000	Share capital	100,000	
27,865	Revenue reserve [3]	44,972	
66,500	Revaluation reserve	66,500	
194,365	Shareholders' funds		211,472
	Amount due and payable in		
80,000	beyond one year		60,000
274,365			271,472

Notes are used with the balance sheet to help you to understand the financial position. They save the balance sheet from becoming too cluttered. Among the most important notes are the make up of:

(a) the fixed assets;

(b) the amounts due and payable in under one year.

Table 1.7: Notes to Bullet Proof Ltd's Balance Sheet

Note 1: fixed assets

	Buildings	Plant	Vehicles	Total
Cost		89,654	43,850	133,504
Valuation	138,990	—	—	138,990
	138,990	89,654	43,850	272,494
Previous depreciation	12,509	44,827	8,770	66,106
Charge for year	1,390	8,965	8,770	19,125
	13,899	53,792	17,540	85,231
Book value	125,091	35,862	26,310	187,263

Note 2: amounts due and payable in under one year

Last year		This year
58,799	Trade creditors	67,554
1,567	Bank overdraft	1,409
20,000	Current portion of long-term debt	20,000
7,174	Accruals	22,306
8,714	Corporation tax	9,436
5,000	Proposed dividend	6,500
101,254		127,205

Note 3: revenue reserve

This year		Last year
12,660	Opening balance	27,865
15,205	Profit retained	17,107
27,865	Closing balance	44,972

Note 4: debtors

Last year		This year
110,549	Trade debtors	118,694
8,514	Prepayments	9,449
119,063		128,143

The corporation tax provision, proposed dividend and retained profit are items covered earlier in the chapter in the profit and loss account.

The Balance Sheet Layout

The balance sheet above is presented in the normal European format. Firstly, the assets are listed in order of realisability. The least liquid are shown at the top, the most liquid at the bottom. Secondly, the short-term borrowings are deducted from the current assets and the resulting total is added to the fixed assets to give the net assets. This total exactly balances with the shareholders' funds plus the long-term debt.

THE CASH FLOW STATEMENT

You saw earlier in the chapter that the profit and loss account gives no indication of whether a business created or consumed cash during the financial year. The balance sheet tells you how much cash a business has but it does not tell you why you have more or less than you had previously. The cash flow statement provides this information. In many businesses the cash flow statement is the most important of the three reports. This is because survival, which corresponds with not running out of cash, is the imperative. There are nine major types of cash flow into a business. There are also nine major types of cash outflow. The cash flows are presented in Figures 1.4 and 1.5 below.

Figure 1.4: Cash Inflows

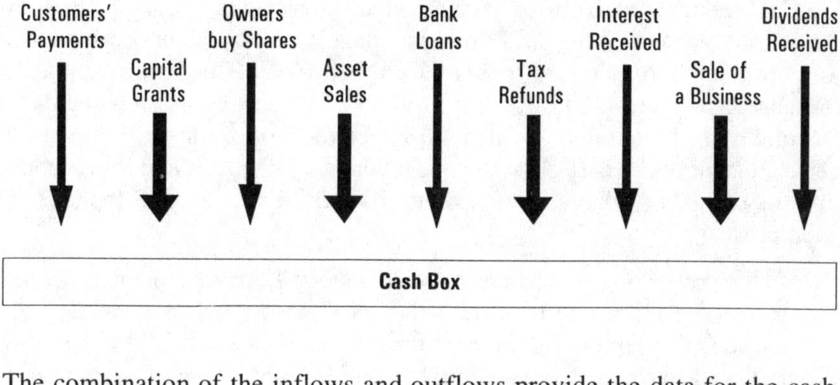

The combination of the inflows and outflows provide the data for the cash flow statement. Unless a business has substantial surplus cash it will need to have larger inflows than outflows. In a seasonal business this will not be the case during the peak. For example, a company that makes Easter eggs would expect to have to make large payments to its suppliers and staff in February of each year. During that month little or no cash would be collected from customers. Fortunately, the cash haemorrhage in the January to March period should be more than compensated in the April to June period.

Figure 1.5: Cash Outflows

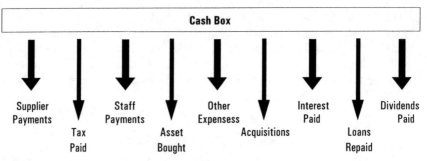

In November 1997, the Accounting Standards Board issued financial reporting regulations for small enterprises, called FRSSE. This encourages small firms to provide a cash flow statement. The standard includes a recommended format in which the cash flows should be reported. The inflows and outflows are summarised in the three major groups given below.

1.   Cash generated from or consumed in operations.

2.   Cash from other sources.

3.   Application of cash.

Explanation for the Categories of Cash Flows

1. Cash generated from or consumed in operations.   This is the most important element of the cash flow statement. It shows the net cash created or consumed in running the business from day to day. This is very important because, as we saw previously, the profit and loss account is prepared on an accrual basis. It does not provide information on the cash flow for the period. This element of the cash flow statement converts the profit and loss account into its cash flow equivalent. There are five major problems in the conversion process.

1.   In the profit and loss account, sales are reported. An adjustment is needed to convert them into their cash flow equivalent. This is necessary because if the debtors increased from the start to the end of the reporting period then the collections from customers will be lower than the sales. Equally, if the debtors fell during the reporting period then the collections from customers will be greater than the sales. The rule is that, in converting the operating profit into its cash equivalent, a decrease in debtors is added or a reduction in debtors is deducted. For example, if a business started the year with trade debtors of £139,605, sold goods or services valued at £528,973 and ended the year with trade debtors of £163,424 the collections from customers would be £23,819 lower than

the sales. You must deduct the £23,819 from the operating profit to convert this element of the profit and loss account to a cash flow basis. This correction to the operating profit pinpoints the additional investment in customer credit. You should check how I arrived at £23,819.

2. In the profit and loss account, purchases are reported. An adjustment is needed to convert them into their cash flow equivalent. This is necessary because if the creditors increased from the start to the end of the reporting period then the payments to suppliers would be lower than the purchases. Equally, if the creditors fell during the reporting period then the payments to suppliers would be more than the purchases. The rule is that in converting the operating profit into its cash equivalent an increase in creditors is added while a reduction in creditors is deducted.

3. In the profit and loss account, operating costs are reported even if they were paid for in a previous or subsequent period. As we saw previously accruals and prepayments are used to calculate the correct profit and loss account charges. These can be substantially different from the cash payments. Adjustments are needed as follows:
    (i)   an increase in prepayments is deducted from the operating profit;
    (ii) a decrease in prepayments is added to the operating profit;
    (iii) an increase in accruals is added to the operating profit;
    (iv) a decrease in accruals is deducted from the operating profit.

    A simple way to understand these rules is to recognise that:
    (a) if assets (debtors or prepayments) rise, then cash falls;
    (b) if they fall, then cash rises;
    (c) if liabilities (creditors or accruals) rise, then cash rises;
    (d) if they fall, then cash falls.

4. Depreciation is charged as a cost in the profit and loss account. Since it is a non-cash charge, it must be added back.

5. Two further distortions can occur. Firstly, if a business makes a profit on the sale of a fixed asset, it will be included in the profit and loss account. However, the full proceeds from the sale must be reported in cash from other sources as we will see later. To avoid a double accounting the profit on sale must be deducted from the operating profit in determining the cash generated from or consumed in operations. Equally, if a business makes a loss on the sale of a fixed asset it will be included in the profit and loss account. However, the full proceeds from the sale must be reported in cash from other sources as we will see later. To avoid a double accounting, the loss on sale must be added to the operating profit in determining the cash generated from or consumed in operations. These adjustments are quite intricate. They need to be mentioned since you will encounter them in any cash flow statement where fixed assets have been sold at prices that are higher or lower than book value.

I think that it is a great pity that the Accounting Standards Board (ASB) did not allow small enterprises to report their cash generated from, or consumed in operations using a direct method format, as they permit for large enterprises. This format reports the cash flows as follows.

• Collections from customers.

• Less payments to suppliers:
   payments to and on behalf of staff;
   payment of other operating expenses.

This format is much easier to understand. The only reservation one might have about it is that it does not specifically point to what is causing the pressure on cash, extra stocks and debtors, as a business grows.

2. Cash from other sources:

(a) interest received;

(b) dividends received;

(c) proceeds from issue of shares for cash;

(d) receipt of capital grants;

(e) receipt of long-term bank loans;

(f) proceeds from the sale of tangible and financial fixed assets;

(g) corporation tax refunds.

3. Application of cash:

(a) interest paid;

(b) dividends paid;

(c) corporation tax paid;

(d) capital expenditure and financial investment;

(e) bank loans repaid;

(f) cash paid to acquire other businesses.

A historic cash flow statement tells you the cash created or consumed in the past. I think the cash flow structure is more useful when it is used to predict inflows, outflows and the cash balance in the future. This is particularly important when a business is growing. The problem with growth is that payments to suppliers and staff will rise long before collections from customers start to improve. The cash forecast tells you that you will run out of money. It gives you time to negotiate a bank loan to tide you over until the crisis abates.

Table 1.8: Cash Flow Statement: Bullet Proof Ltd

Last Year		This year	
	Cash generated from operations		
39,534	Operating profit	41,546	
18,143	Depreciation	19,125	
2,839	(Increase) decrease in stocks	(14,853)	
(16,484)	(Increase) in debtors	(8,145)	
(826)	(Increase) in prepayments	(935)	
6,322	Increase in trade creditors	8,755	
(3,493)	Increase in other creditors	15,132	
46,035			60,625
	Cash from other source		
2,364	Interest received		1,464
	Application of cash		
(12,403)	Interest paid	(9,967)	
(6,935)	Taxation	(8,714)	
(12,690)	Capital expenditure	(15,000)	
(4,000)	Equity dividends paid	(5,000)	
(20,000)	Term loan repayment	(20,000)	(58,681)
(7,629)	Increase / (decrease) in cash for year		3,408
21,957	Cash less overdrafts at the start of the year [1]		14,328
14,328	Cash less overdrafts at the end of the year [1]		17,736

Note 1: Reconciliation of opening and closing cash

Opening cash	15,895	Closing cash	19,145
Less overdraft	(1,567)	Less overdraft	(1,409)
Net cash at start of year	14,328	Net cash	17,736

Note 2: Direct method operating activities (not required by the FRSSE)

Collections from customers	518,844
Payments to suppliers	(198,338)
Payments to and on behalf of staff	(86,143)
Payments for other expenses	(173,738)
	60,625

Commentary on the Bullet Proof Ltd Cash Flow Statement

For a small company, Bullet Proof Ltd generated a strong cash flow from operating activities. Collections from customers at £518,844 exceeded the cost of running the business from day to day by £60,625. Part of this cash was used to:

(a) pay interest on money borrowed £9,967;

(b) pay last year's corporation tax £8,714;

(c) acquire new fixed assets £15,000;

(d) pay the dividend proposed at the last AGM £5,000;

(e) repay a term loan instalment of £20,000.

In particular the acquisition of additional fixed assets and the reduction in bank debt strengthened the business. Taking all the inflows and outflows into account, Bullet Proof ended the year with £17,736 in net cash resources. This was an improvement of £3,408 on the position at the start of the year.

Interpretation of the Cash Flow Statement

There are two crucial issues in the interpretation of a cash flow statement. Firstly, it is vital to have a net cash inflow from operating activities. Without this there will be no money to meet the non-discretionary outflows, such as interest and tax payments and loan repayments. Secondly, it is not necessarily bad to have an overall reduction in cash for a period. This should occur when an organisation has too much cash and is diverting it into activities that will provide an attractive future return. For example, Bullet Proof Ltd ended last year with net cash resources of £17,736. It could certainly permit the bulk of this to be used for business development initiatives in the next year. This issue will be examined in Chapter 11, where we look at the use of the cash flow statement format to measure the implications of the strategic plan for future cash resources.

SUMMARY

Financial statements provide the basis for checking the financial health of a business. The profit and loss account measures profitability. It tends to be the statement that attracts the most attention from shareholders. There are two vital issues involved in understanding a profit and loss account.

1. It covers a period of time. The period is one year for financial accounts. It should be one month or a quarter for management accounts. In order to

judge whether the actual results are satisfactory they should be compared against a budget.

2   The profit and loss account compares the sales with the costs relevant to the period. There is a popular misconception that it is a cash document. It is not.

The balance sheet provides information on the things that a business owns (assets) and how the assets are financed. It provides much of the information used to test the effectiveness of management. For example, it is easy to carry too much stock 'just in case'. To do so is a costly luxury. Unlike the profit and loss account, the balance sheet paints a picture at a point in time. The balance sheet could be hugely different from one month to another, particularly in a seasonal business.

Cash is to a business as blood is to a human being. If the heart of the business fails to pump enough of it, the business will die. The inflows and outflows of cash are divided into two main groupings: the operational (day to day) cash flows and the business development cash flows. If a business is growing the outflows may exceed the inflows. A business may try to grow too fast and run out of cash.

Appendix One

The Profit and Loss Account of a Manufacturing Business

The profit and loss account of a manufacturing business is more difficult to prepare and interpret than that of a trading one. The primary reason is that the cost of production must be computed. This requires calculation of the value added to the raw materials used in production. The books of Peter Plant provide the following information for last month.

Purchases of materials (net of VAT)		85,000
Production labour		48,653
Other factory costs		39,465
Sales		234,265
Non-production costs		29,642
Stocks	**Start of month**	**End of month**
Raw material	14,265	15,469
Work in progress	7,193	6,134
Finished goods	18,400	17,200

Profit and loss account Peter Plant Ltd

Opening stock of raw materials	14,265	
Purchases	85,000	
Materials available for use	99,265	
Closing stock of raw materials	15,469	
Issues to production	83,796	
Production labour	48,653	
Factory expenses [1]	39,465	
Decrease in work in progress	1,059	
Cost of production [2]	172,973	
Sales		234,265
Opening stock of raw materials	18,400	
Cost of production	172,973	
Cost of producing goods for sale	191,373	
Closing stock of raw materials	17,200	
Cost of sales		174,173
Gross profit		60,092
Selling and administration costs [1]		29,642
Profit before interest and tax		30,450

[1] Substantial detail may be provided in management accounts.

[2] Equivalent to purchases in a trading organisation.

Valuation of work in progress and finished stock can be difficult. The following example shows the approach. Stephen Straw builds houses. Each house takes twelve weeks to construct. Stephen and his staff start and complete one house every working week. His estimator computed the cost of a completed house.

Site and services	42,000
Materials	24,000
Labour	18,000
Site expenses	12,000
	96,000

Stephen has agreed to value and report his work in progress and finished stock to his bank each week. To help in this valuation his surveyor estimates the degree of completion of each house under construction. The following is the stock valuation at the end of last week.

House	Site	Material Input %	Value	Labour Input %	Value	Site Expenses	Total
1	42,000	20	4,800	7	1,260	1,000	49,060
2	42,000	35	8,400	15	2,700	2,000	55,100
3	42,000	40	9,600	22	3,960	3,000	58,560
4	42,000	45	10,800	32	5,760	4,000	62,560
5	42,000	50	12,000	40	7,200	5,000	66,200
6	42,000	55	13,200	47	8,460	6,000	69,660
7	42,000	60	14,400	54	9,720	7,000	73,120
8	42,000	65	15,600	61	10,980	8,000	76,580
9	42,000	70	16,800	68	12,240	9,000	80,040
10	42,000	78	18,720	75	13,500	10,000	84,220
11	42,000	87	20,880	86	15,480	11,000	89,360
12	42,000	100	24,000	100	18,000	12,000	96,000
	504,000		169,200		109,260	78,000	860,460

This valuation is not significantly different from one based on an assumption that each house was 50 per cent complete. The valuation would then be:

Site 42,000 x 12	504,000
Materials 12,000 x 12	144,000
Labour 9,000 x 12	108,000
Site expenses 6,000 x 12	72,000
	828,000

Such a valuation might be acceptable for management accounts but not for audited accounts.

Appendix Two

The Valuation of Financial and Intangible Fixed Assets

These valuations are among the more complex areas in accounting. The rules are in a state of flux. In November 1997, the ASB issued FRS9 and FRS10. FRS9 deals with the valuation of associated companies and joint ventures. It applies to accounting periods ending on or after 23 June 1998. However, the standard specifically exempts small entities. They are still covered by the previous legislation, contained in SSAP1. The major issues in valuation of investments under SSAP1 are as follows. Investments are categorised in three groups.

1. **Those that confer control.** The test of control is normally that the investor holds more than 50 per cent of the shares and voting rights. In such cases consolidated or group accounts are required. In these accounts the investment is replaced with the underlying assets and liabilities. If the group does not own all the shares in the investee, then a minority interest must be recorded and reported. If the price paid to acquire the business is more or less than the underlying net assets then goodwill arises. Minority interests and goodwill are illustrated in the following example.

    Dada Ltd paid £1.8 million for 75 per cent of the shares of Baba Ltd. At the time of the acquisition Baba Ltd had net assets of £1.1 million. The £1.8 million purchase consideration, for a 75 per cent shareholding, valued Baba Ltd at £2.4 million. As a consequence the goodwill was £1.3 million (excess of purchase consideration over the net asset value) and the minority interest was £0.6 million (25 per cent of the net assets of Baba Ltd including goodwill).

2. **Those that confer significant influence.** The general test of significant influence is the entitlement to play a major role in operating and financial policies. When an investor holds between 20 per cent and 50 per cent of the shares in another business it will be presumed to have significant influence. Nevertheless, each investment will be examined and judged on its merits. Where significant influence is deemed to exist the investor must prepare group accounts. In the group profit and loss account, the share of profit is recorded and the underlying tax liability deducted. In the group balance sheet, the investment is shown at cost: a) plus the investors share of the accumulated retained profit since the shareholding was acquired, or b) minus the investors share of the accumulated losses since the shareholding was acquired. For example, Large Ltd bought a 40 per cent stake, 40,000 shares at the nominal value of £1 per share, at the inception of a joint venture. Suppose that in the year

after purchase the joint venture company summarised profit and loss account was as follows.

Operating profit	13,680
Corporation tax	4,100
Retained profit	9,580

Firstly, Large Ltd will bring its £5,472 share of the profit of associate into its profit and loss account. Secondly, it will include its £1,640 share of the corporation tax liability in its profit and loss account and balance sheet. Thirdly, it will add £3,832 to the value of its investment.

3. **Simple investments.** The stake is too small to confer control or significant influence. Only the dividend income from these investments is recorded in the investors profit and loss account. The investment is normally shown at cost in the investors balance sheet. However, if the investment has turned out to be ill judged it should be marked down to its economic value and the loss reported in the profit and loss account.

FRS10 deals with the valuation of intangible fixed assets. It applies to accounting periods ending on or after 28 December 1998. However the standard specifically exempts small entities. They are still covered by the previous legislation, contained in SSAP22. By far the most important intangible fixed asset is purchased goodwill. FRS10 requires that it be carried as an asset in group accounts and amortised over its useful life, normally twenty years or less. SSAP22, the predecessor to FRS10, permits two ways of treating goodwill. It can be: a) carried as an asset in group accounts and amortised over its useful life, normally twenty years or less, or b) cancelled against shareholders funds. Small firms that have acquired another business and paid a goodwill premium are probably wisest to cancel the goodwill against reserves. The major reason for this is that their bankers will almost certainly redraft the accounts to exclude goodwill when calculating gearing. The issue of goodwill and its effect on gearing is discussed in detail in Chapter 5.

I find it quite incongruous that the accounting standards board should introduce new rules for valuation of investments in FRS9 and for valuation of intangible fixed assets in FRS10 and then continue to encourage the application of the old rules for small entities. In particular the fact that the FRSSE was issued just before FRS9 and FRS10 makes the exemption quite surprising. Surely if the new rules are logical for larger businesses they must also be logical for smaller ones. In fairness both standards imply that the new valuation rules will be applied to smaller entities when the FRSSE is revised at some future date.

CHAPTER 2

ANALYSING FINANCIAL STATEMENTS: THE DIAGNOSIS

In Chapter 1 I helped you to understand the financial statements of your business and the accounting conventions used in preparing them. These statements portray the health or sickness of your business. It is not enough to understand the financial statements, you must also be able to search within the figures and diagnose strengths and weaknesses. Key relationships, called ratios, provide the basis for this diagnosis. Ratios identify weaknesses in the statements that need to be attacked and strengths that can be capitalised on. The ratios are of three major types:

- tests of profitability;

- tests of financial stability;

- tests of the effectiveness of working capital management.

The Profit and Loss Account Under the Microscope

TESTS OF PROFITABILITY

1. Gross Margin: This ratio tests the effectiveness of manufacturing or trading operations. The data is taken from the profit and loss account. The ratios for our company Bullet Proof Ltd are shown in Figure 2.1.

Figure 2.1: The Gross Margin

	Last year	This year
Gross Margin	112,124	141,278
Sales	324,997	448,501
Margin %	34.5	31.5

Last year out of each pound of sales Bullet Proof spent 65.5p on making the product for sale. This left 34.5p to pay for overheads and to divide between the stakeholders. This year the gross margin fell to 31.5 per cent. The 3 per cent decline in the margin is serious. The cost of producing its product for sale rose more quickly than the prices at which it sold to customers. Was this caused by increased competition in the business sector? If it was, can Bullet Proof cope with further competitive pressure? If the cause of the decline is inefficiency, can Bullet Proof find a way to eliminate it, and restore the margin to the previous level? There is no doubt that the board of Bullet Proof should be aware of the decline in this margin. They should also understand the reason why it occurred, and have taken steps to rectify the problem. Unlike some of the later ratios, the gross margin should be computed and examined at each board meeting. Early awareness of pressure on the margin should lead to prompt action to address it.

2. The Pre-tax Margin: This ratio tests the effectiveness of overall operations. The relevant data is contained in the profit and loss account. The ratios for Bullet Proof are shown in Figure 2.2.

Figure 2.2: The Pre-tax Margin

	Last year	This year
Profit before tax	28,919	33,043
Sales	324,997	448,501
Margin %	8.9	7.4

This ratio measures overall profitability. Not surprisingly, the pre-tax margin also declined. The haemorrhage was not as serious as that at the gross profit level. As we will see later, the sales grew by 38 per cent. I would expect the overheads to increase more slowly than the sales as the company improved the utilisation of its support costs. This appears to have happened and it alleviated some of the damage that occurred at the gross margin level. Nevertheless, the decline in pre-tax margin remains disturbing.

3. The Profit Before Interest and Tax Margin: One of the most revealing uses of ratios is to provide a comparison with a relevant competitor. Such benchmarking can sometimes prove misleading. The pre-tax margin is a ratio that is unsuited to benchmarking. Consider two businesses that sell similar volumes of similar products at similar prices and are equally efficient. The only significant difference between the two businesses is that one has a large bank debt and relatively small shareholders' funds, whereas the other has no bank debt and relatively large shareholders' funds. The pre-tax margin should be higher for the company with no bank debt. This is because there is no interest to be charged in its costs. The higher margin in the company should not be assumed to be because of greater efficiency, it simply emerges as a result of a different financing strategy. For benchmarking purposes this difficulty can be overcome by comparing the margin before interest (operating margin) with the sales. The ratios for Bullet Proof are shown in Figure 2.3.

Figure 2.3: The Pre-interest and Tax Margin

	Last year	This year
PBIT	39,534	41,546
Sales	324,997	448,501
Margin %	12.2	9.3

This provides a more reliable basis for benchmarking. The 2.9 per cent decline in the profit before interest and tax (PBIT) also tells us that the major reason for the improved pre-tax margin was a reduction in the interest cost. The saving came as a result of a lower amount of interest bearing borrowings.

4. Asset Turns: The first three ratios used in this analysis provide insights into the ability of management to squeeze profit out of sales. They only tell part of the story of management effectiveness. Another vital test of effectiveness is the ability to squeeze sales out of assets. When these two tests of effectiveness are combined, we get an overall picture of profitability that is called return on investment (ROI). This will be dealt with in ratio 5 on page 30. Before we do so we will calculate the asset turns. There are computed by comparing the sales with the total assets (fixed + current) see Figure 2.4.

Figure 2.4: Asset Turns

	Last year	This year
Sales	324,997	448,501
Total Assets	375,619	398,677
Turns	0.87	1.13

The ability of Bullet Proof to squeeze sales out of assets improved significantly in the current year. This may have resulted from improved utilisation
of fixed assets (for example, machines working longer hours), or improved
utilisation of current assets (for example, manufacture of stock closer to point
of sale or speedier collection of amounts due from customers). We can break
down the turns to help us establish which is the case in Figures 2.5 and 2.6.

Figure 2.5: Fixed Asset Turns

	Last year	This year
Sales	324,997	448,501
Fixed assets	191,388	187,263
Turns	1.7	2.4

Figure 2.6: Current Asset Turns

	Last year	This year
PBIT	324,997	448,501
Current assets	184,231	211,414
Turns	1.76	2.12

This more detailed analysis shows that the utilisation of both fixed and current assets improved significantly. When we analyse the working capital we
will explore whether the improved current asset turns was caused by faster
stock turnover or improved debt collection. Asset turns can vary dramatically from one business to another. Consider the assets and turns of the following sectors.

Sector	Commentary	Turns
Forestry	Trees: the fixed assets take years to grow	0.05
Airport	Runways: expensive compared to landing fees	0.6
Construction	Work in progress very large	0.5
Manufacturer	Expensive machines + high current assets	0.8
Wholesaler	High current assets	1.5
Department store	High stocks and low debtors	3.0
Supermarket	Fast stock turns and low debtors	10.0

In all sectors the asset turns will be lower if the properties are owned than if
they are leased.

5. Return on Investment: This ratio combines the PBIT (operating) margin with the asset turns to provide an overall picture of management effectiveness. The Bullet Proof ROI is shown in Figure 2.7.

Figure 2.7: Return on Investment

	Operating margin	x	Asset turns	=	ROI
Last year	12.16%	x	0.87	=	10.53%
This year	9.26%	x	1.13	=	10.42%

In spite of the large reduction in operating margin, the decline in ROI is minimal. This is due to the greatly improved asset turns. Any business should set a 10 per cent ROI as the minimum goal. In some business sectors a 10 per cent ROI can be achieved through high margins and low asset turns. In other sectors, low margins will be acceptable because high asset turns can be achieved. These variations in margin are driven by competition. A sector with low assets is easy to enter and will attract a lot of competition. A sector with high assets is hard to enter (it requires too much shareholder investment) and will attract much less competition. Return on investment is the key to contented shareholders. If a business can borrow funds at 6 per cent and invest them at 10 per cent the 4 per cent difference is earned for the shareholders. It will lead to an attractive return on equity as we will see in ratio 6.

6. Return on equity: This ratio compares the profit earned on behalf of the shareholders with their investment in the business. It can be calculated before, or after, corporation tax. I favour the before tax approach. It facilitates comparison with return on investment and tests the effectiveness of borrowings. The pre-tax return on equity of Bullet Proof is shown in Figure 2.8.

Figure 2.8: Return on Equity (pre-tax)

	Last year	This year
Profit before tax	28,919	33,043
Shareholder's funds	194,365	211,472
ROE %	14.9	15.6

The average cost of borrowing by Bullet Proof is lower than the return on investment. Last year an ROI of 10.5 per cent led to an ROE of 14.9 per cent. This year an ROI of 10.4 per cent led to an ROE of 15.6 per cent. Figure 2.9 shows how this happened.

Figure 2.9: The Impact of Debt on ROE

PBIT	–	Debt service cost	=	PBT
Total assets	–	Total debt	=	Shareholders' funds
=		=		=
ROI		Average cost of debt		ROE
Last year				
39,534	–	10,615	=	28,919
375,569	–	181,254	=	194,365
=		=		=
10.5%		5.9%		14.9%
This year				
41,546	–	8,503	=	33,043
398,677	–	187,205	=	211,472
=		=		=
10.4%		4.5%		15.6%

Last year Bullet Proof borrowed £181,254 at an average cost of 5.9 per cent, and invested it at 10.5 per cent. This low cost debt pushed the return on equity to 14.9 per cent. This year a debt service cost of 4.5 per cent lead to an ROE of 15.6 per cent. It is important to realise that, if the return on investment is lower than the average service cost of debt, interest will destroy the return on equity. For example, see Figure 2.10.

Figure 2.10: Destroying ROE

PBIT	–	Debt service cost	=	PBT
Total assets	–	Total debt	=	Shareholders' funds
=		=		=
ROI		Average cost of debt		ROE
24,000	–	15,000	=	9,000
400,000	–	200,000	=	200,000
=		=		=
6%		7.5%		4.5%

The shareholders would have earned an ROE of 6 per cent if no debt had been used. The 7.5 per cent servicing cost of the debt damaged the ROE and destroyed shareholder value. Return on equity can also be measured after tax. The after tax ratios for Bullet Proof are shown in Figure 2.11.

Figure 2.11: Return on Equity (post-tax)

	Last year	This year
Profit after tax	20,205	23,607
Shareholders' funds	194,365	211,472
ROE %	10.4	11.2

Many analysts regard this measure as more meaningful. It is certainly fair to argue that corporation tax inevitably follows profitability. Nevertheless, the deduction of tax spoils the test of effectiveness of borrowings.

Financial Stability

The second element of ratio analysis tests financial stability. There are two major ratios: gearing and interest cover.

7. Gearing: This tests the relationship between the bankers' loans to a business and the owners' investment in a business. The greater the bank proportion in this mix, the more the bank will be at risk. For this reason, bankers regard gearing as the primary test of financial stability. This being the case, it is incumbent on a business to protect their relationship with their bankers by not taking on excessive debt. The big problem is that an entrepreneurial bank manager may allow a business to run up excessive debt. If they are replaced by a conservative manager, that person may force their corporate customer to sell assets to rectify the excessive gearing. The most saleable assets are likely to be the most profitable ones. To sell such assets, to bring gearing back to a sensible level, can wreak havoc with the prospects for future profitability. The gearing of Bullet Proof is quite conservative (see Figure 2.12).

Figure 2.12: Gearing

	Last year	This year
Long-term bank debt	80,000	60,000
Short-term bank debt	20,000	20,000
Bank overdraft	1,567	1,409
Less cash	(15,895)	(19,145)
Net bank borrowings	85,672	62,264
Shareholders' funds	194,365	211,472
Gearing %	44.1	29.4

Collection of the net bank borrowings can prove challenging. They will include: overdrafts, term loans, mortgages and lease obligations. The gearing of Bullet Proof declined significantly. The major reason was the strong cash flow. This enabled the repayment of a £20,000 term loan instalment, while still leaving a £3,408 increase in cash.

A good guideline is that gearing should not exceed 100 per cent. However, I believe that a wise business will not allow gearing to exceed 80 per cent. This is because unexpected opportunities to invest attractively sometimes arise. For example, a business with shareholders' funds of £100,000 and net bank borrowings of £80,000 has the capacity to borrow an additional £20,000, without letting the gearing go out of control. There are two situations where a bank may tolerate excessive gearing:

(a) a promising new business that is short of an adequate capital base;

(b) a management buy-out.

In both situations, the bank will require tight restrictions on management salaries and dividends so that the hoped for strong cash flow will enable the gearing to rapidly decline to an acceptable level.

In the late-1980s, many banks allowed their corporate customers to gear too high. The recession that followed resulted in the inability of many such businesses to create the strong cash flows that they needed to restore an acceptable level of gearing. Sadly, this led to the liquidation of many businesses that had promising potential. Gearing will be discussed further in Chapter 5.

8. Interest cover: The other major test of financial stability is interest cover. Interest cover tests the capacity of a business to pay interest and to repay bank debt, whereas gearing represents the level of security available to bankers if a business fails.

It is a sad fact that most businesses start life with too little owners' capital and too much bank debt. Tight limits on salaries and dividends in the early years should help such businesses to create substantial positive cash flows. Retention of these earnings helps to 'beef-up' the shareholders' investment while allowing a reduction in bank debt. Unfortunately, large interest bills can destroy the ability to create surplus cash and the business can die in infancy. The interest cover of Bullet Proof is shown in Figure 2.13.

Figure 2.13: Interest Cover

	Last year	This year
Profit before interest	39,534	41,546
Interest	10,615	8,503
Cover	3.7	4.9

In the current year the interest cover of Bullet Proof improved significantly.

In both years it substantially exceeded the minimum sought by banks. This minimum, a cover of at least three times, will be discussed in Chapter 5.

Many books on business finance spend a lot of time discussing two other aspects of financial stability: the current ratio and the liquidity ratio. These are, in my opinion, less important than gearing and interest cover. The current ratio compares the current assets with the amounts due and payable in under one year. A current ratio of less than one is undesirable. This is because the value of stocks and debtors that will be turned into cash will not be sufficient to repay the short-term liabilities as they fall due. The liquidity ratio excludes stock from the current assets when comparing them with the amounts due and payable in under one year.

9. Working Capital: The term 'working capital' is loosely and, in my opinion, unsatisfactorily defined by many accountants. For the purposes of this book working capital is defined as:

Stocks + Trade Debtors – Trade Creditors

As a business grows, it will need to hold more stocks to support the expected extra sales and have to give extra credit to its customers. This growth in operating assets can cause problems with the cash position. Fortunately, the fact that the business is buying or producing more goods should lead to extra supplier credit. This eases some of the pressure on cash.

The size of working capital investment, which is necessary to support sales, varies significantly from one sector to another. For example, a business that sells fresh fruit and vegetables must operate a just in time (JIT) stocking policy, whereas a builder of office blocks will have a large investment in work in progress. Equally, a dairy will collect from its door to door customers once a week, whereas a supplier of fertilisers to farmers can only expect to collect when the crop is harvested and sold. It is for these reasons that the working capital needs vary dramatically from sector to sector.

The overall working capital investment should be measured as a percentage of sales. The ratios for Bullet Proof are shown in Figure 2.14.

Figure 2.14: Working Capital Ratio

	Last year	This year
Stocks	49,273	64,126
Trade debtors	110,549	118,694
Trade creditors	(58,799)	(67,554)
Net working capital	101,023	115,266
Sales	324,997	448,501
Shareholders' funds	31.1	25.7

The working capital of Bullet Proof, expressed as a percentage of sales, declined by 5.4 points in the current year. Nevertheless, it remains high. The reasons for this are the long stock holding period and the customer credit period, which will be examined in the next two ratios. For the moment the implication of the working capital ratio is that, if sales were to rise by £100,000 next year, Bullet Proof would need additional cash resources of £25,700 (25.7 per cent of sales) to finance them. Without these extra funds, Bullet Proof would be exposed to the deadly virus of overtrading (discussed in Chapter 3). If Bullet Proof wishes to improve its capacity to fund expansion, it will need to find ways to make or buy stocks closer to the point of sale and to collect from customers more quickly.

10. Stock turnover: Large stocks are an expensive luxury for any business. They are a corporate version of obesity. Two major issues make such obesity very costly. Firstly, if the average value of stock investment of a firm is £100,000, it will cost at least £20,000 a year to hold it. This is made up of:

• space costs, such as rent, rates, light and heat;

• security costs, such as insurance and stock control;

• interest on the money borrowed to pay for the stock.

Secondly, such stock is exposed to risks of deterioration and obsolescence. For these reasons JIT became a management priority in the 1980s, and remains so in the 1990s. Many businesses still seem to maintain that JIT is only workable in industries that trade in perishable goods or those that outsource large quantities of components for predictable volumes, e.g. cars or computers. Nevertheless, the really professional small businesses have organised themselves, and their suppliers, to acquire goods closer to the point of sale.

The stock turnover ratio illustrates the effectiveness or ineffectiveness of the stocking policy. The Bullet Proof holding period is shown in Figure 2.15.

Figure 2.15: Stock Holding Period

	Last year	This year
Stocks	49,273	64,126
Average monthly cost of sales (1)	17,739	25,602
Stockholding period (months)	2.8	2.5
(1) 212,873		307,223
12	= 17,739	12 = 25,602

These ratios indicate that Bullet Proof shortened the turnaround time for its stocks significantly, but should be seeking further improvement.

Sometimes businesses measure stock holding in slightly different ways.

Days, weeks, turns and percentages provide the same information. The fact that Bullet Proof improved stockholding will be revealed by whichever method of computing and expressing it is used.

11. Collection period: The gap between the point of sale and the date of collection from credit customers, places a huge strain on cash resources in some businesses. A wise business will monitor this gap, often called the average collection period, carefully, though measurement is sometimes difficult. The problem being that sales are reported net of VAT and must be compared with trade debtors, which are reported including VAT. We will examine how to cope with this distortion later. For the present we will examine the figures for Bullet Proof, a company that exports all of its products and is not required to charge VAT to its customers. The average collection period of Bullet Proof is shown in Figure 2.16.

Figure 2.16: Average Collection Period

	Last year	This year
Trade debtors	**110,549**	**118,694**
Average monthly sales (1)	27,083	37,375
Average collecting period (months)	4.1	3.2
(1) **324,997**		**448,501**
12	= 27,083	12 = 37,375

Collections from customers improved significantly. Benchmarking the average collection period against relevant competitors should indicate whether Bullet Proof has further scope for improvement.

If all the sales of Bullet Proof were in the home market and customers were charged an additional 17.5 per cent VAT, the average collection period would have to be computed by grossing up the sales or netting down the debtors. The collection period of Bullet Proof would have to be amended as shown in Figure 2.17.

Figure 2.17: Average Collection Period (VAT)

	Last year	This year
Trade debtors	**110,549**	**118,694**
Average monthly sales (1)	31,823	43,916
Average collecting period (months)	3.5	2.7
(1) 27,083 + 17.5% = 31,823. 37,375 + 17.5% = 43,916		

A wise manager will compute the average collection period regularly from management accounts. If the sales pattern is seasonal, then you should calculate the collection period by dividing the sales of the last three months by three. Comparing this calculation of relevant average monthly sales with the debtors reveals the quarterly average, which is more meaningful than the annual average. If using this measure of the average collection period, it is better to compare the ratio with the same month last year rather than with the previous month.

12. Growth trends: These are obtained by comparing figures from year to year. For example the sales of Bullet Proof rose by £123,504. This was a 38 per cent increase on the previous year sales of £324,997. Figure 2.18 shows the key trends.

Figure 2.18: Growth trends

Sales	+38.0%
Cost of sales	+44.3%
Gross profit	+26.0%
Overheads	+37.4%
Pre-tax profit	+14.2%
Stocks	+30.1%
Trade debtors	+7.4%
Trade creditors	+14.9%

Sales are the fulcrum of growth. The sales rose by 38 per cent. The trend analysis shows that the cost of sales rose faster at 44.3 per cent. This lead to a gross margin, increase of only 26 per cent. Overheads increased faster than the gross margin at 37.4 per cent. This left a disappointing increase in the pre-tax margin of only 14.3 per cent. The improved stock turnover and average collection period noted in ratios 10 and 11 are confirmed by the growth analysis. A 7.4 per cent increase in trade debtors on the back of a 38 per cent growth in sales is particularly impressive.

THE USE OF RATIO ANALYSIS IN YOUR BUSINESS

1. Ratios should be applied to budgets as well as to historic results. If the ratios computed in the budget are not satisfactory, it pinpoints weaknesses in the plan. You should prepare and interpret the ratios in all budgeted and historic financial statements.

2. In order to avoid overloading you with data, I presented you with only two years of ratios for Bullet Proof. To prepare a detailed picture of the trends in a business, you need at least five years of ratios. Graphs of the ratios can be very informative. The use of spreadsheets makes this a

straightforward task. It should be greatly appreciated by your board of directors.

3.   Spreadsheet modelling can take the drudgery out of five-year calculations.

4.   Ratios are of most use to a manager when they are properly benchmarked. For example, it would not make sense to compare the stock turns of a supermarket with those of a house builder. It is often difficult to locate a relevant benchmark. Size and product mix are major factors that make location of an appropriate benchmark difficult.

SUMMARY

To be an effective manager, you must be able to diagnose any problems with the finances of your business. You can do this by preparing and interpreting ratios. These ratios test the effectiveness of management in:

(a)   squeezing profit out of sales;

(b)   squeezing sales out of assets;

(c)   not allowing the debts to become excessive.

Ratios should be prepared when budgets have been drafted. They pinpoint the appropriateness of your plan in terms of profitability, financial stability and asset utilisation. There are three key questions that ratios answer.

1.   Will the sales less the costs provide adequate profits?

2.   Can the assets be appropriately funded to provide financial stability?

3.   How effective is your plan for management of operating assets (stocks and debtors)?

If the profits are inadequate, the liabilities excessive or the stocks or debtors are too high, the budget is inappropriate and should be revised.

CHAPTER 3

You Can Sell Too Much!
The Temperature Test

It may seem surprising, but a business can try to sell too much. You can have selling prices, sales volumes and costs right and still run out of cash. Cash is the lifeblood of any organisation. Lack of it can cause your business to run a dangerously high temperature. The problem can creep up on your business when cash inflows are smaller than cash outflows, and can even happen in very profitable businesses. The major cause of the problem is that, in most businesses, customers expect to buy on credit. Consequently, the suppliers and staff have to be paid long before the money is collected from customers. The business is exposed to the often fatal condition called overtrading. The business runs out of cash and dies at the hands of the liquidator.

Figure 3.1: Cash Flow

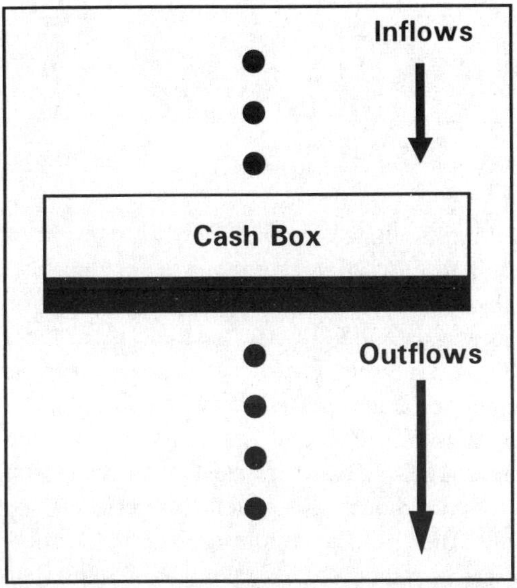

Tom Stretch was about to set up a small wholesale business. A friend, who was an accountant, advised him to prepare a forecast of the cash that would flow in and out of the business in the first year of trading. Tom expected to sell 20,000 units per month at £5 each, starting in February. He would buy each unit for £4. He planned to buy about two weeks before sale to cater for possible delays in delivery and buoyant demand. His supplier would direct debit Tom's bank account in the month after purchase. Tom expected that one half of each month's sales would be paid for by customers two months later, with the balance being collected a further month later. He forecast that other cash costs of the business would be £5,000 in the first month and £14,000 per month thereafter. He put £100,000 of his own money into the business and persuaded his bank to allow him a £100,000 overdraft. Table 3.1 shows his cash forecast for the first six months.

Table 3.1: Example Cash Forecast for Tom Stretch

£'000

Month	Jan	Feb	Mar	Apr	May	Jun	Total
Cash introduced	100	–	–	–	–	–	100
Collections	–	–	–	50	100	100	250
	100	–	–	50	100	100	350
Suppliers		40	80	80	80	80	360
Other costs	5	14	14	14	14	14	75
	5	54	94	94	94	94	435
Monthly balance	95	-54	-94	-44	6	6	-85
Opening cash	–	95	41	-53	-97	-91	
Closing cash	95	41	-53	-97	-91	-85	

Sales in the first three months exceeded Tom's wildest dreams. He was sure that the profits he had earned were much greater than the £13,000 he had budgeted, even though his other costs, particularly deliveries, were higher than expected. He was astounded when the bank manager telephoned to say that he had deferred payment of a direct debit from his supplier pending immediate lodgement of at least £40,000. On receipt of this amount, the bank would be in a position to meet the payment. Since Tom had no prospects of collecting this amount from customers, he asked his supplier not to represent the direct debit for one month, by which time collections from customers would enable him to meet it. The supplier refused. A receiver was appointed and the business was promptly sold. Tom received more than he had invested when the receiver distributed the proceeds from the sale. This was of little consolation. He had lost a business that had made a profit of £59,766 in the four months that he owned it. Tom's company succumbed to the deadly virus called overtrading. If he had sold less he would still own a prosperous business. Tables 3.2 and 3.3 tell the story of his actual cash receipts and payments and his profits for the four months in which he traded.

Table 3.2: Actual Cash Inflows and Outflows

Month	Jan	Feb	Mar	Apr	Total
Capital	100,000	–	–	–	100,000
Collections	=	=	7,044	84,884	91,928
	100,000	=	7,044	84,884	191,928
Suppliers	–	20,000	66,000	167,000	253,000
Other costs	8,366	17,894	19,265	21,636	67,161
	8,366	37,894	85,265	188,636	320,161
Balance	91,634	-37,894	-78,221	-103,752	-128,233
Opening cash	=	91,634	53,740	-24,481	
Closing cash	91,634	53,740	-24,481	-128,233	

Table 3.3: Actual Profit and Loss Account

Sales		634,635
Purchases	576,000	
Less stock	68,292	
Cost of sales		507,708
Gross profit		126,927
Overheads		67,161
Net profit		59,766

Tom had bought 144,000 units and sold 126,927 units. The profits were superb, but the cash position was disastrous. This sad story is an everyday occurrence in business. The same as many an owner manager, Tom learned the hard way that you can sell too much. It sounds extraordinary but the reason is simple. A continuous cycle is operating in any business that sells a product or service. In Tom's business there is a fifteen week gap between the purchase of goods for sale and final collection from customers. He must pay his staff and suppliers long before he recovers these costs from customers. Tom failed to understand the operating cycle of his business.

The more Tom sold the greater his need for cash. This should have tided him over, from the point of paying suppliers and staff to the point of collect-

Figure 3.2: The Operating Cycle

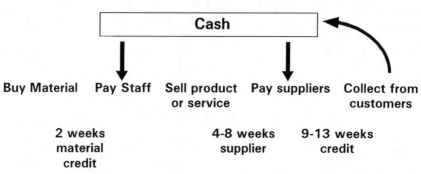

ing from customers. It was Tom's failure to understand this that caused him to lose his profitable business. If a business is profitable, suppliers and banks sometimes tolerate growing indebtedness, in the belief that the situation will rectify itself when volume stabilises. The trouble is that they sometimes lose patience and take steps to close down their errant customer. Tom was unlucky. His financiers should have been more tolerant. Could Tom have persuaded them to support him if he had changed his plans to meet the increased customer demand? Possibly. They would have had to be highly skilled and entrepreneurial.

A manufacturing business often has a longer operating cycle than the fifteen weeks illustrated above. The principal reason is that it needs to hold three types of stock: raw material, work in progress and finished goods. A wholesale or retail business usually has a shorter cycle since suppliers normally finance the stock. If you run a service business, you might think you hold no stock. However, you could be wrong. For example, a software development business must pay staff to create their product long before they start collecting from customers. The cash cost of this work in progress can be difficult to fund. The principles developed in this chapter and in the outline operating cycle given above, apply to most businesses. Financial institutions and supermarkets are major exceptions. For other businesses, the major issue is the length of the operating cycle and the amount of cash resources required to fund it.

One of the troubles in finance is that accountants, like all professionals, use terms not properly understood by non-experts. Firstly, while the term 'trade debtors' certainly means money due from customers, it also represents money that has been used to pay suppliers and staff to create the product or the service you supply. A major reason why Tom's cash position deteriorated is that £542,707 was due from customers. This was far more than the £250,000 that Tom had predicted. Secondly, non-experts tend to think of stocks solely as an asset, whereas they also represent cash paid to suppliers and staff that has not yet been recovered from customers. When the business failed, Tom's stocks were £28,000 higher than he had predicted. The start-up was very profitable. The tragedy is that Tom ran out of cash. Too much cash was consumed in the operating cycle which I define as.

Stocks + Trade Debtors – Trade Creditors

Failure to raise sufficient funds, from owners and bankers, caused the business to fail in infancy.

Cash planning is a vital financial tool for a business that is starting up or growing rapidly. It does not require professional accounting training to predict how much cash will flow into and out of your business in the next six months. Without this knowledge you could run out of cash, just as Tom did. Adequate cash is far more important than profitability in such cases. Failure is more likely to be caused by running out of cash than by incurring a loss. Tom expected to sell 60,000 units and earn a profit of £13,000 in the first four months of trading. He actually sold 126,927 units and made a profit of £59,766, but his business ran out of cash. The cash required to fund the operating cycle strangled the profitable business. Your overtrading crisis could be caused by a different factor than Tom's. For this reason it is vital that you understand what causes overtrading and how to avoid this dangerous disease.

THE SEVEN CAUSES OF OVERTRADING

1. The prime cause is trying to sell more than your cash resources permit.

2. A variation on this occurs when a business starts to sell another product. The new product will create another operating cycle. New product introductions also require expenditure on design and market development. New funds for development must be arranged because the cash already available is required to support the current product(s).

3. Dramatic examples of overtrading occur when a business incurs losses. Unless volumes fall dramatically, the collections from customers will be less than the payments required to run the business on a day to day basis.

4. Failure to arrange funds to pay for new investment, in vehicles, buildings and equipment can put undue pressure on your cash. I know of one business that could have collapsed because the owner bought an expensive car using money soon to be needed to pay the staff and suppliers. Fortunately for him, he asked me to solve his cash problem. I persuaded his understanding bank manager to refinance the car on an (expensive) lease. This released cash to pay the operating costs. Exercising an 'attractive' option to acquire a premises, previously rented, is frequently the cause of falling into the overtrading trap. It is often relatively easy to

arrange a mortgage to cover about 80 per cent of the cost, but do not use the working capital to pay the other 20 per cent.

5. Inability to collect from customers on time is another way into an overtrading crisis. In Tom's start-up example, the cash situation would disimprove if customers delayed settlement for a further month.

6. Another mistake that can lead to an overtrading crisis is to allow stocks to grow too high. Certainly it is a serious sin to fail to land a profitable sale through lack of stock. Equally, opportunities occur to buy stock just before a supplier introduces a major price increase. Both issues will help to improve profits, but may dramatically worsen the cash position.

7. A price increase by a supplier can also lead to overtrading. Suppose that Tom had to buy at £5 and sell at £6, his forecast of the cash position would deteriorate, as shown in Table 3.4.

Table 3.4: Cash Forecast for Tom Stretch when Overtrading

£'000

Month	Jan	Feb	Mar	Apr	May	Jun	Total
Cash introduced	100	–	–	–	–	–	100
Collections	–	–	–	60	120	120	300
	100	–	–	60	120	120	400
Suppliers	–	50	100	100	100	100	450
Other costs	5	14	14	14	14	14	75
	5	64	114	114	114	114	525
Monthly balance	95	-64	-114	-54	6	6	-125
Opening cash	–	95	31	-83	-137	-131	
Closing cash	95	31	-83	-137	-131	-125	

PRESCRIPTIONS FOR OVERTRADING

There are three prescriptions that help to prevent an overtrading crisis:

1. financial;

2. pricing;

3. credit.

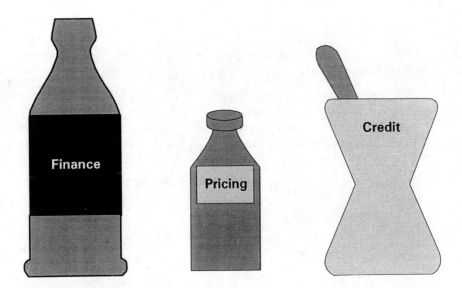

The Financial Prescriptions

1. *Introduce enough owners' investment.* Firstly, sufficient capital must be raised. Secondly, the owners should retain some of the profits so as to contribute to the higher funds required in the operating cycle when volumes are growing. Excellent cash forecasts will pinpoint the funds required. Many potential entrepreneurs find it hard to amass sufficient funds to enable their business to start life with a healthy cash balance. If the promoter's funds are inadequate, it is wise to try to attract a partner, who can help to provide an adequate capital base, rather than to start life with insufficient funds.

2. *Negotiate bank facilities before you need them.* A banker expects three things when a customer seeks additional loans:
    (a) a well-documented forecast of why the funds are required;
    (b) an explanation of how long the funds will be required for and how they will be repaid;
    (c) time to assess the assumptions and projections and if necessary to refer the loan application to a higher authority within the bank.

    Given these three things, a request for additional funds will usually receive a positive response. If, on the other hand, a company chooses to continue to write cheques in the full knowledge that if the bank is to cash them the borrowing limit will be exceeded, it will be playing a very dangerous game. At best this corporate version of Russian roulette will be met by punitive interest charges. At worst it will lead to 'bounced' cheques and a damaged reputation.

3. *Arrange to buy stock just in time for production and make stock just in time for sale.* JIT would save Tom £40,000 in cash. Many companies still believe that JIT cannot work in their industry. Most of my clients have changed their minds about this hypothesis in recent years.

4. *Avoid unnecessary costs.* In my experience, a significant amount of spending in most businesses provides poor value for money. Avoiding wasteful costs can take significant pressure off the cash requirements as well as providing additional profits (this issue will be dealt with in detail in Chapter 10). The point is that excessive cost can lead to overtrading.

5. *Finance your assets correctly.* Stocks and debtors are more important than flashy cars and luxurious premises. It may be possible to finance the status symbols later, when volumes level off.

The Pricing Prescriptions

1. *Decide to sell at a higher price.* If Tom decided to sell at £5.50 per unit he would probably:
   • sell less;
   • have a more comfortable cash position;
   • earn higher profits.

2. *Try to buy at lower supply prices.* The fact that your output is growing means that your suppliers should be experiencing economies of scale. It is reasonable to argue that costs, such as order processing and delivery, should be declining on a per unit basis. If Tom could get a reduction of 25p per unit, he would add £25,000 to his six-month profit forecast. This would occur because he would save 25p per unit on the cost of the 100,000 units that he hoped to sell. He would also hope to save £22,500 of his precious cash as a result of the reduction of 25p from each of the units he would have to pay for.

The Credit Prescriptions

1. *Negotiate improved settlement terms with suppliers.* An extra month of supplier credit would save the fledgling company £80,000 in cash and significant bank interest.

2. *Set shorter customer credit terms.* A start-up business should set tight terms for customer credit. This sets the standard for future collections and limits the risk of unrealistic credit expectations. It is difficult to change credit terms once a business is established and to retrain customers into earlier settlement. Some companies introduce settlement discounts to assist the retraining process. I am strongly opposed to them for two rea-

sons. Firstly, amounts, such as 2 per cent cash discount for settlement within seven days, are much more expensive than they sound. For example, if a customer buys £1,000 per day and pays one month after purchase, a shift to seven-day settlement will release £23,000 from the debtors but will cost £7,300 per annum (365 days at £1,000 per day multiplied by 2 per cent) This is an annual cost in excess of 31 per cent. Secondly, customers who already settle promptly will take the discount. Slow payers will not be able to afford early settlement and, furthermore, some of them will have the cheek to try and take the discount when settling in their usual dilatory fashion.

3   *Chase customers for settlement when accounts become due.* To allow settlements to fall even two weeks behind has a disastrous effect on the cash position. A sensible organisation will prepare an age analysis. This pinpoints customers who should be chased.

How not to manage an Overtrading Crisis

There are three incorrect ways to attack an overtrading crisis.

1.   Try to take excessive and unauthorised credit from suppliers. These suppliers will quickly recognise that the account is overdue. They can wreak havoc by placing a stop on further supplies and (or) by commencing recovery actions.

2.   Decide to delay payment of amounts due to the tax authorities. The trouble with this strategy is that the Inland Revenue will charge interest on the overdue tax.

3.   Decide to play 'I dare you bounce' with the bankers. They can and will return your cheque unpaid. They might even seek a liquidation.

The Core Issue in avoiding Overtrading

The best way to avoid an unacceptable cash position is to forecast your future cash inflows and outflows as accurately as possible. It is easy to write a spreadsheet model that paints a picture of the cash position for at least six months in advance. The model should be updated to reflect the actual sales and costs and their inflow and outflow implications as each month passes and to extend the forecast by a further month, so as to stay six months ahead.

The Exception proves the Rule

Some businesses make all, or most of, their sales for cash and hold little or no stock. Provided the other elements of good financial planning and control are implemented, there should never be a cash crisis. The more they sell, the better will be their cash position. The good news for such businesses is that they cannot overtrade unless they diversify into areas that have an inbuilt delay between payments to create or acquire their product or service and recoup the cash from their customers.

Things to remember when preparing a Cash Forecast

The key inputs for a cash forecast are the expected collections from customers and payments to suppliers and staff. The predicted collections from customers will be based on the sales forecast. Account must be taken of the gap built in by the terms and conditions of sale. Furthermore, patterns of settlement quickly develop which help the manager to predict the fast, medium and slow payers. If you wish to be as accurate as possible, and have a small number of customers, you can build a subsidiary spreadsheet that shows the sales and collections on a customer by customer basis. Most organisations will use their history of collection to forecast inflows, such as:

- 40 per cent collected in month after sale;

- 35 per cent in second month after sale;

- 25 per cent in the third month after sale.

Supplier payments are based on predicted purchases and normal delays pre-settlement. Payments to, and on behalf of, staff are reasonably predictable.

- When and how much basic pay will be paid?

- When and how much PAYE and social insurance will be paid?

- How much overtime will be worked?

- What will it cost and when will it be paid?

There is a danger that other cash flows can be overlooked because they are less frequent. For example:

1. Some operating costs, such as insurance, must be paid in advance.

2. Other operating costs, such as bank interest, will be paid in arrears.

3. Tax on the profits of the business are payable in arrears.

4. Dividends to shareholders may be paid once or twice a year.

5. Equipment and vehicles will be purchased and paid for occasionally and don't forget the proceeds from the sale of old plant and vehicles.

6. Commitments to repay loans will have to be met.

7. Payments for leases must be made.

8. Receipt of loans must be planned and recorded.

9. If share issues for cash are to be made they must be recorded as must the expenses incurred in such fund-raising.

10. The takeover of another business for cash must be recorded.

SUMMARY

A major problem for growing businesses is that it is possible to run out of cash. This can happen even when a business is very profitable. The core issue is that suppliers and staff have to be paid long before the sale proceeds are collected from customers. The thermometer test shows that the bank debt is higher than was authorised and that the business is overtrading. To avoid catching this illness the wise proprietor will do three things.

1. Predict the cash flows for at least six months ahead.

2. Avoid waste in the operating cycle (customer credit and stock).

3. Ensure that investments are correctly funded. This is dealt with in Chapter 9.

CHAPTER 4

KNOW HOW YOU STAND:
THE BLOOD PRESSURE TEST

In large companies it is standard practice to prepare monthly management accounts. These compare actual performance with a predetermined budget. In small companies the preparation of monthly accounts is rare. The astute owner manager realises that sales, wages and cash are the things that can vary significantly and need to be carefully monitored. Sales are usually the most volatile of the three variables. In many small companies, these are monitored using a graph that is updated weekly and displayed in a prominent position. The budget is also plotted in the graph. The owner-manager is elated when the position looks like Figure 4.1.

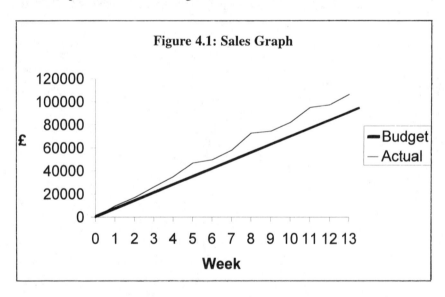

Salaries and wages are also carefully monitored in small companies. Indeed they are often quite stable from week to week and month to month. The astute owner-manager realises that overtime is the factor that stops them from being totally predictable. They watch the overtime bills like the proverbial hawk.

Adequacy of the cash, which is available to pay bills as they become due, is also a priority in small companies. The moving six-month forecast, which I advocated in Chapter 3, is the way to ensure that there are sufficient funds available to meet obligations as they fall due.

Management of the three pressure points (sales, wages and cash) is a reasonable effort at control. Unfortunately, it is not enough as you move towards the 21st century. It may sound surprising but when an organisation sells even two products, usually with different gross profit margins, it is possible that the total sales could exceed budget, while the total profits could be very disappointing. This would arise when sales of the product with a low gross margin, were ahead of budget and sales of the product with a high gross margin, were behind budget. You can imagine how poor an indicator of profitability the sales are when an organisation sells hundreds of different products.

To be in control an organisation needs four pieces of financial information.

1. A monthly profit and loss account that compares sales and costs against the budget.
2. An aged list of debtors that pinpoints debtors that are paying too slowly.
3. A stock control system that shows the volume and value of all significant lines.
4. A rolling six-month cash forecast.

The profit and loss account is particularly important. I do not believe that a chief executive can claim to be in control if a monthly profit and loss account is not prepared. Changes in demand, selling prices and costs, can occur so rapidly that it is not acceptable to wait even three months for a financial update, and yet many businesses do not know how they have performed until after the annual audit has been completed.

When a doctor examines a patient who is not feeling well, the blood pressure is one of the tests they use. The profit and loss account is to a business like the blood pressure gauge is to a human. It must be checked regularly. The management accounts are the mechanism for checking it.

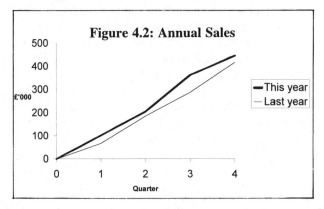

Bill Carfix runs a small service station. His bookkeeper records all purchases, sales, cash receipts and payments and sends bills to credit customers. Neither Bill nor his bookkeeper have the confidence or experience to prepare a regular profit and loss account for the business. However, Bill feels he is doing well. His barometer of progress is sales. If they exceed the weekly target, Bill is confident that he is making money. A graph on the wall in his office suggests that this year was the best ever for the service station.

Figure 4.2: Annual Sales

Bill recently sent the books to his auditor to prepare the annual accounts. Imagine his surprise when the auditor told him that the profit for last year was £33,464. This was a great disappointment compared to the previous year when £43,652 was earned. When he examined the profit and loss account, he found that the sales were up as expected. The summarised results were as in Table 4.1.

Table 4.1: Example Profit and Loss Account for Bill Carfix

	This year			Last year		
	Forecourt	**Workshop**	**Total**	**Forecourt**	**Workshop**	**Total**
Sales	298,243	149,122	447,365	250,478	166,985	417,463
Cost of sales	254,384	114,079	368,463	209,939	120,742	330,681
Gross margin	43,859	35,043	78,902	40,539	46,243	86,782
Overheads			45,438			43,130
Profit			33,464			43,652

Bill was horrified. He realised, for the first time, the importance of product mix. Sales in the more profitable workshop had fallen, whereas sales on the less profitable forecourt had risen. Furthermore, the auditor pointed out the fact that gross margins had declined substantially in both sections (see Table 4.2).

Table 4.2: Gross Margins

	This year	**Last year**
Forecourt	14.7	16.2
Service	23.5	27.7

The best that Bill could hope for was that he could reverse these unfavourable trends in the future. The moral of this story is that to be in control, regular financial statements must be prepared and reviewed. If Bill had done this, the change in mix and the decline in margins would have been identified quickly and Bill might have been able to counteract them. The lesson probably cost Bill £10,000 that he, and his business, could ill afford.

PREPARING THE PROFIT AND LOSS ACCOUNT

If you accept that a monthly profit and loss account is a vital document, then you must decide who is to prepare it and how quickly you need it. It may be possible to find a retired accountant who would work for half a day each month to prepare it. Failing this, you or your bookkeeper can take on the task. A possible short cut is available. What is this short cut and why is it so interesting?

In accounting, costs can be classified in two types:

(a) costs that rise and fall in response to volume (called variable costs);

(b) costs that remain similar regardless of volume (called fixed costs).

The fixed costs are time-based and you should be able to predict them accurately. Classic examples of time-based costs are rent and rates. Indeed, the application of accruals and prepayments to fixed costs tends to provide a spurious and unnecessary accuracy. If you have prepared a reliable fixed cost budget, then you can simply divide it by twelve and have a sensible figure to deduct from your gross profit. However, you should remember that mistakes can be made in the budget, and that circumstances that drive costs can change. For these reasons, I recommend that you should have a full accrual based profit and loss account prepared at least quarterly.

Considering this, you should have concluded that it is the gross profit section that is volatile and needs to be carefully monitored. There are four major issues that together determine the gross profit:

- the volume of sales;

- the selling prices;

- the product mix;

- the cost of production or procurement.

The computation of gross profit is so important that I am going to review the measurement of sales and cost of sales even though these were covered in Chapter 1. Consider the following questions.

1. Last month the value of goods and services supplied to customers totalled £31,308. The cash collected from customers was £29,110. Which figure will be used as sales in the profit and loss account?

2. Last month Bill Carfix bought 54,000 litres of petrol at 55p per litre, and sold 52,180 at 60p per litre. What will be the cost of petrol charged against sales in the profit and loss account?

Answers to Profit and Loss Questions

1. The sales figure is £31,308. The value of goods and services he supplied is reported. This must exclude VAT. Businesses simply charge VAT to customers and pay the proceeds to the tax authorities. The fact that the collections from customers were £2,198 less than the sales, simply means that the cash receipts are disappointing.

2. In this trading business, the cost of petrol sold is reported under the heading 'cost of sales'. Provided that the price of petrol has not changed since the previous month and there are no stock shortages, Bill will charge £28,699 against sales. Bill should carry out a stock check before preparing his accounts. The trading account would be reported as in Table 4.3, if no stock was missing.

Table 4.3: Example Trading Account for Bill Carfix

Sales[1]		31,308
Purchases [2]	29,700	
Less stock [3]	1,001	
Cost of sales		28,699
Gross margin		2,609

[1]52,180 litres at 60p.
[2]54,000 litres at 55p.
[3]1,820 litres at 55p.

Why is the stock valued at only 55p when it can be sold for 60p? Because the FRSSE requires that stock must be valued at the lower of cost or net realisable value. This is part of the general principle in accounting that you do not anticipate profit until it is earned.

Preparation of the gross profit is more difficult in a manufacturing business. You need to calculate the production expenses as well as the direct material and direct labour. The short cut approach can help you with part of the production overhead calculations. You need to be careful to apply it only to the fixed costs. The variable costs must be computed accurately. For example, if the sales volume is higher than budget, then you should expect that the cost of packing materials will also exceed budget. Energy is another important variable cost in many manufacturing businesses. Variable costs must be measured accurately using stock adjustments, accruals and prepayments where necessary.

INTERPRETING THE MONTHLY PROFIT AND LOSS ACCOUNT

When the monthly profit and loss account has been prepared, the actual outcome will inevitably be different from the budget. Volume sales of some products or services may be higher than budget, while others may be lower. The effective chief executive must be able to identify the cause(s) of sales variances and the actions that need to be taken to counteract adverse ones. Equally the cost of production or procurement can be significantly different from the budget. Once again the manager must be able to diagnose the cause(s) of variances, and to decide on appropriate actions to overcome them.

The key issue in budgetary control is that, in spite of inevitable and unexpected variances, a business must deliver the profit it has targeted. To do so requires that appropriate recovery actions are taken when variances occur. As well as reporting performance for the previous month, year to date figures must be presented. These will show how the business has progressed for the year so far. These figures are particularly important when there have been significant adverse variances in previous months. In such circumstances, meeting the budget for the current month will not be sufficient to compensate for a shortfall experienced previously.

Computerised Bookkeeping and Accounting Systems

Many businesses keep their accounting records by computer. Good software packages simplify the preparation of a monthly profit and loss account. Whether you use a manual or computerised bookkeeping system, good judgement is required to ensure that all transactions are recorded and reported correctly. If you find that a transaction is difficult to record or report, then you should check it with your auditor.

Table 4.4: Trading and Profit and Loss Account for the Month of January

	Budget		**Actual**		**Variance**
Sales		25,000		23,869	(1,131)
Opening stock	1,250		1,853		
Purchases	13,500		12,448		
	14,750		14,301		
Closing stock	1,250		1,689		
Cost of sales		13,500		12,612	888
Gross profit		11,500		11,257	(243)
Administration	3,645		3,830		(185)
Selling	3,150		3,095		55
Delivery	3,865		3,607		258
Operating expenses		10,660		10,532	128
Operating profit		840		725	(115)
Interest		240		215	25
Profit before tax		600		510	(90)
Corporation tax		200		170	30
Profit after tax		400		340	(60)
Gross profit per cent		46.00		47.16	
Operating profit per cent		3.36		3.03	

Sales in January were a disappointing 4.5 per cent below budget. Savings arose because of the lower purchasing caused by the decline in sales and a reduction in overtime in the warehouse and on the delivery truck. The principal goal for next month is to recover the lost sales ground. In February sales will need to exceed budget by at least £1,131. The February report should show the planned and actual results for the year to date, as well as those for the month. This should pinpoint the effectiveness of the actions taken to recover the ground lost in January. Each month after that, the year to date results will show the progress towards the annual profit target.

The gross margin improved as a result of improved stock control and pricing. The net margin declined because the cost savings were not sufficient to offset the decline in gross profit. This usually happens when sales fall because many of the costs relate to time (fixed) and not to volume (variable). If the volume cannot be recovered, it will be necessary to carry out some cost surgery since a lower volume of sales cannot support this level of overhead.

Why you may not need a Balance Sheet

A balance sheet shows the assets of a business and the funds that enabled these assets to be owned. Most of the items do not change significantly from month to month. You can monitor the items that do vary without preparing a balance sheet.

1. You need an aged listing of the amounts due from customers. This will pinpoint the amounts overdue that need to be chased. For example:

Customer	Current	1 Month	2 Months	3 Months +
D Readful	946.73	827.64	922.71	1,911.26

    The £1,911.26 is seriously overdue and should be vigorously chased.

2. Stock can also gobble up cash. It needs to be tightly controlled. Every business needs a stock control system. The system should be tested by regular sampling. A good system will quickly highlight the size and cost of pilferage. It will also draw attention to slow-moving stock.

3. You also need a schedule of amounts owed to suppliers and the times when payments will fall due. Failure to pay on time can result in a stop on supplies. This could seriously disrupt production and customer delivery schedules.

Table 4.5: A 'Short Cut' Profit and Loss Account Illustration

	April			4 Months to end April		
	Budget	**Actual**	**Variance**	**Budget**	**Actual**	**Variance**
Sales	85,000	88,635	3,635	340,000	338,193	(1,807)
Cost of sales	52,700	51,190	1,510	210,800	209,113	1,687
Gross profit	32,300	37,445	5,145	129,200	129,080	(120)
Payroll[1]	14,125	14,863	(718)	59,409	58,604	805
Overhead [1]	13,900	13,900	–	55,600	56,045	(445)
Total exes.	28,045	28,763	(718)	115,009	114,649	360
Profit	4,255	8,682	4,427	14,191	14,431	240
Gross margin %	38.0	42.2		38.0	38.2	
Net margin %	5.0	9.8		4.2	4.3	

[1] The company uses a 'short cut' approach to accounting for overheads. That is why no variance is shown for April. A full profit and loss account had been prepared for the first three months. The owner expected that the overspending for the first three months would not be repeated.

April saw a substantial recovery after three difficult months. Sales were 4.3 per cent ahead of budget. Several production savings helped to improve the gross margin from 38 per cent to 42.2 per cent. The year to date sales are now only £1,807 behind the budget as compared with £5,442 for the previous quarter. Gross profit is now £120 behind budget as compared to £5,265 at the end of March. Overall, the April results are a triumph for all those involved in implementing recovery actions. Profits are now marginally ahead of budget compared with a shortfall of £4,187 at the end of March. If the recovery actions had not been taken, then the company would face a decline in profit of more than £16,000 for the year. This would have been very serious for a company of this size.

SUMMARY

Customer demand and profitability can decline owing to circumstances that may not be capable of being rectified. The simplest form of control is to compare the sales for the year to date with the budget and with the same period last year. While this provides good indicators of progress, it is not sufficient in the modern business. Product mix can change or costs can spiral without the owner realising it. You need a regular profit and loss account to test the blood pressure and pinpoint the problems quickly. It will highlight the need for corrective action. Waiting for the auditor to prepare the accounts allows too much time to elapse before the necessary corrective action is taken.

If you cannot afford a full-time or part-time accountant to prepare the results, then you, or your bookkeeper, will have to do it. It should not prove too difficult, particularly if you follow the short cut approach I advocate in this chapter. When preparing a profit and loss account the following major points must be observed.

1. Income is the value of goods or services billed to customers, net of VAT.

2. Cost of sales must be computed. This requires accurate valuation of stock.

3. In computing the costs, to be charged against income, you must make appropriate accruals and prepayments. These arise due to the fact that payments are made at different times from when the costs are incurred.

4. If the business makes a profit, you must decide whether part of this must be earmarked (appropriated) to cover future corporation tax or dividend payments.

CHAPTER 5

FINANCIAL STABILITY: THE ELECTROCARDIOGRAPH

Financial stability should be the primary goal of any business. As I outlined in Chapter 2, it is best measured by calculating gearing and interest cover. These measures are so important to financial health that I will explore how to calculate and interpret them correctly in this chapter. Financial stability is at the heart of any business. Gearing and interest cover are the equivalent of an electrocardiograph.

One of the greatest problems that a business can face is to owe too much money to its bankers. In accounting jargon, this is called excessive gearing. The business is committed to large payments of interest and capital. This is not a problem when a business is doing well. It becomes difficult when economic conditions deteriorate and insufficient cash is being generated to repay the capital and interest obligations. The bank can lose confidence and recall the loan or appoint a receiver, liquidator or administrator.

Too steep for top gear

Anne Bigger ran a highly successful business that distributed floor tiles to retailers and house builders. One year ago a Swedish manufacturer of fitted kitchens asked her to sell its product. Anne liked the proposal. The same distribution channels, in which she had superb contacts, would be used to sell both sets of products. Furthermore, the Swedish supplier offered sole distribution rights, excellent margins, subvention of initial marketing costs and four months' credit. Anne decided to sell the fitted kitchens.

Sales in the first year substantially exceeded the targets Anne had set herself. Early in the second year Anne ran into serious trouble with her bank. The bank manager was not prepared to increase her company borrowing limit and large cheques were due to both the floor tile and fitted kitchen suppliers. Anne felt that the bank were being unreasonable, since her monthly accounts showed that the business had more than doubled the profit of the previous year.

She decided to try and move her account to a different bank. She prepared a prospectus for her business and presented it to two other banks in the area. Both were highly impressed with the achievements and prospects for the business but were not prepared to meet her borrowing requirements. Each said that the proposed gearing was too high. One of the bankers suggested that she talk to their venture capital subsidiary and she did this. The reaction of the venture capitalist was very positive. Their representative offered to invest £500,000 in exchange for a 40 per cent shareholding and to ensure that the business could draw down sufficient loans as were required to meet the current and future operating needs of Anne's business. While the offer was very tempting, Anne turned it down. She hated the idea of sharing her business with a bank, and particularly disliked the requirement that they would be allowed to appoint two directors to the company board. Anne decided to struggle on.

Anne now faced a series of angry meetings with suppliers. She was finally given a choice between closing down or selling an 80 per cent stake to the Swedish kitchen supplier for £400,000. She reluctantly returned to the venture capitalist and said she had decided to accept this offer. Unfortunately, he said that he had used up his investment resources for the current year and suggested that Anne come back to talk to them in six months. Ten days later, with all options exhausted, Anne accepted the £400,000 offer from the Swedish company, and lost 80 per cent of her business. She continues to work for the company but is disillusioned by the unfair treatment meted out to her by the banks and her Swedish supplier.

What should Anne have done? Before deciding to sell fitted kitchens she should have arranged funding for the second operating cycle. If this proved impossible, she should have stuck to her successful floor tile business.

If a modern day Moses brought financial commandments to the business community, number one would be 'thou shalt not gear too high'. Had Anne known about and lived by this commandment she would still control a profitable and prosperous business.

WHAT IS GEARING?

Gearing is the relationship between the money invested in a business by the owners and the money lent to a business by the bankers. The higher the proportion of bank funds in this 'cocktail' the greater the risk to which a bank is exposed. Gearing is calculated by extracting and comparing two aspects of the business from its balance sheet (see Table 5.1).

Table 5.1: Net Bank Borrowings – Shareholders' Funds

Gearing	Low	Medium	High	Imminent Collapse
Net bank borrowings	300	650	1,500	4,000
Shareholders' funds	1,200	1,000	1,000	800
Gearing per cent	25	65	150	500

A business proprietor must be able to calculate gearing correctly. A wise business will calculate not just the historic gearing from an actual balance sheet but also the prospective future gearing from a budgeted balance sheet.

How to calculate Net Bank Borrowings Correctly

1. The short-term bank borrowings are taken from the liabilities due and payable in under one year section of the balance sheet.

2. The medium-term and long-term bank borrowings are taken from the liabilities due and payable beyond one year section of the balance sheet.

3. Any cash shown in the current assets is deducted from the total for short, medium and long-term borrowings.

Computing this total is not always as easy as it might sound. Mortgages, debentures, loan stocks and bonds are all forms of bank or quasi-bank debt. They must be included when calculating net bank borrowings. An interesting example of the problems associated with calculating net bank borrowings correctly arose some time ago in a large, Irish company. This group bought another business three days before the end of the financial year. Payment for the acquisition *circa* £29 million would not become due for about six weeks to allow time for a 'due diligence' review. The £29 million consideration was correctly described in the amounts due and payable in under one year as 'other creditors'. A superficial examination of the gearing might overlook the fact that this would become bank debt in about six weeks and it should be taken into account. When you analyse the financial stability of a business, you should watch out for this type of snag.

It might seem surprising, but obligations to make repayments of the capital element of finance leases must also be included in calculating gearing. The reason for this is that lease obligations are similar to term loan repayments. SSAP21 requires that the assets and obligations associated with a finance lease must be shown in the balance sheet of the lessee (user). This rule was introduced because many businesses were using finance leases as an artificial contrivance to conceal debt.

Measuring Shareholders' Funds (Different Perspectives)

In Chapter 1 we saw that shareholders' funds are of three types:
- share capital;
- undistributed profits (revenue reserves);
- revaluation reserve;

A good board of directors will ensure that when a business is growing that enough of the profit is retained so as to help fund expansion without letting gearing become excessive (see Table 5.2).

Table 5.2: Comparative Gearing Levels

		One year later	
	Start-up	**Sensible**	**Dangerous**
Assets	100	250	250
Financed by:			
Share capital	60	60	60
Retained earnings	–	90	–
Bank loans	40	100	190
	100	250	250
Gearing	66.6	66.6	316.6

A successful start-up could run into excessive gearing if all the profits are paid out as dividends. A prudent board protects the financial stability by persuading shareholders to retain some of the profits. This strengthens the capital base as the assets grow. Note how this example is linked to the increased funds required for the operating cycle (as developed in Chapter 3).

Owners sometimes have a major investment in a business that they fail to fully recognise. Consider a simplified example. A consortium of speculators expect that a piece of agricultural land will inevitably get drawn into suburbia as the nearby city expands. They invest £1 million to buy the land. They then lease it to the previous owner, who continues to farm it. The lease charge exactly equals the running costs of the consortium. Five years later the land is re-zoned to residential and the consortium feel they can make a killing by developing it. The snag is that it would cost £4 million to service the land and build houses. No bank would be prepared to lend the consortium the £4 million on the basis of the existing balance sheet. To do so would allow a gearing of 400 per cent. However, it is reasonable to argue that showing the land in the balance sheet at cost is seriously misleading. The consortium obtained a valuation of £5 million from a highly respected auctioneer. They restated the balance sheet as follows.

	£million
Land at valuation	<u>5</u>
Share capital	1
Revaluation reserve	<u>4</u>
Shareholders' funds	<u>5</u>

They then approached the bank showing a prospective gearing of 80 per cent. Is it reasonable to argue that the owners have invested £5 million? The auditors would certainly give a 'true and fair' certificate to such a balance sheet. This example highlights an important principle of good business practice. A wise business will recognise that 'as time passes' the value of appreciating assets, such as land and buildings, can become understated. To disclose these assets at too low a value can have three adverse consequences:

(a) the gearing appears higher than it really is;

(b) the full potential to borrow on the strength of the balance sheet is not recognised;

(c) an unwanted takeover bid could arrive based on the assumption that the owners did not realise the true value of their business.

It is sensible to revalue appreciating assets about once every five years.

GOODWILL AND ITS EFFECT ON GEARING

The treatment of goodwill is one of the most controversial aspects of accounting. It can have a major impact on gearing. Goodwill can arise when one business acquires another. What usually happens is that the buyer believes that the balance sheet of the seller fails to recognise certain intrinsic qualities, such as the quality of the products, the loyalty of the customers and the calibre of the management. If the buyer makes a successful offer at a price that is higher than the stated value of the net assets, goodwill arises. The new group must produce a consolidated balance sheet. The directors have two options as to how the goodwill is treated. It can either be included as an asset or deducted from reserves. Consider the following example. Dada offered £5 million in cash for Baba which has net assets of £1 million. The offer was accepted. On completion of the acquisition, the group balance sheet is prepared by adding the assets and liabilities of the two parts (see Table 5.3).

Table 5.3: Example Group Balance Sheet for Dada and Baba

	Dada	Baba	Goodwill	No Goodwill
Goodwill	–	–	4,000	–
Fixed assets [1]	15,650	675	11,325	11,325
Cash	100	50	150	150
Other current assets	6,785	3,187	9,972	9,972
Overdraft	(2,250)	(412)	(2,662)	(2,662)
Other payable under 1 year	(1,246)	(2,500)	(3,746)	(3,746)
	19,039	1,000	19,039	15,039
Term loans [1]	6,750	–	6,750	6,750
Share capital	3,000	250	3,000	3,000
Reserves	9,289	750	9,289	5,289
	19,039	1000	19,039	15,039
Gearing			75.4%	111.7%

[1] The balance sheet of Dada was prepared after the company bought and paid for Baba. It includes an investment in Baba valued at £5 million and a loan of the same amount. To prepare group accounts the investment in Baba is cancelled against its capital and reserves. The difference of £4 million is goodwill. If it is shown as an asset, the balance sheet is as headed goodwill. If it is deducted from reserves, the balance sheet is as headed no goodwill.

The important point about the alternative treatments is that when goodwill is deducted from reserves, the gearing passes the danger level of 100 per cent. Debate about the treatment of goodwill continues. Some commentators argue that it is a very real asset and that to exclude it is misleading. Others argue that it is a view of a business at a moment in time and that the value can change dramatically as economic and sectoral conditions alter. They believe that it should not be disclosed as an asset. Suffice to say that conservative businesses will cancel the goodwill against reserves, thus showing these reserves, and consequently the gearing, at a higher level than those that choose to treat it as an asset. Since most bankers choose to revise their client balance sheets to exclude goodwill, the conservative approach is the best indicator of borrowing potential. As mentioned in Chapter 1, the cancellation of goodwill against revenues will not be allowed for larger entities in accounting periods ending on or after 28 December 1998.

WHY BANKS REGARD MORE THAN 100 PER CENT AS DANGEROUS

Banks use gearing to measure the security for loans to corporate customers. Their major concern is ability to recover the loan if the business fails. A liquidator will repay the liabilities in the following order:

1. preferential creditors;

2. secured creditors;

3. unsecured creditors.

4. shareholders.

Since bank loans are usually secured, the fact that unsecured creditors and shareholders are later in the queue appears to offer good protection. There are two snags. Firstly, when a business fails the assets rarely realise their balance sheet value. The lower amounts realised undermine the apparent security. Secondly, a liquidation gives rise to preferential creditors. Redundancy payments, liquidator's fees and certain taxes are examples. Experience has shown bankers that a gearing in excess of £1 of net bank borrowings for each £1 of owners' funds leaves them dangerously exposed.

SEASONAL IMPACT ON GEARING

Many businesses have highly seasonal sales. A dramatic example is a business that makes Easter eggs. In the months before Easter, the company will spend heavily to buy the materials and make the eggs. By the end of June the customers should have paid for their eggs and the company should be in a strong cash position. Because the funds required to build the stocks and to give credit to customers are only needed for a short time, the company should use overdraft funding.

Two things are important about planning financial stability in such an industry. Firstly, the financial year should end after the peak season sales have been collected from customers and, secondly, the company, its suppliers and bankers should be aware of the fact that the gearing is portrayed at the most favourable time. A smart analyst can make a good estimate of the peak gearing as follows.

	Amount	**Period**
Interest received	8,650	7 Months
Interest paid	12,650	5 Months
Probable borrowing rate	10%	

Peak borrowing is approximately 12,650 / 10 per cent x 12 / 5 = £303,600.

THE ROLE OF A BANK IN RESTORING FINANCIAL STABILITY

When a business allows its gearing to rise to an uncomfortable level, its bankers become concerned. In order to help restore the gearing to a sensible level banks often suggest that assets should be sold. The problem is that the ones likely to be most saleable are the ones from which the best profits are earned. Disposal of assets will certainly lower the gearing but this is achieved by damaging the potential to earn adequate profits in the future. The only way to avoid forced sales of the best assets is to keep gearing under tight control. Knowing the impact on gearing of proposed investments in fixed and current assets is the key to keeping it under control.

Another Aspect of Security for Bankers

Good bankers are more interested in a long-term relationship with a growing and profitable business than they are with security in the case of failure. The best test of the ability of a corporate customer to provide this stable relationship is called interest cover. Interest cover is:

$$\frac{\text{Profit before Interest and Tax}}{\text{Interest}}$$

To understand why interest cover is so important to a bank, we must first consider why a business needs a profit. Consider Table 5.4.

Table 5.4 Breakdown of Company Profits

Company	A	B	C
Sales	365,123	244,875	583,122
Cost of sales	310,354	167,293	425,654
Gross profit	54,769	77,582	157,468
Overheads	40,075	55,541	120,733
Profit before interest and tax	14,694	22,041	36,735
Interest	7,347	7,347	7,347
Profit before tax	7,347	14,694	29,388
Taxation	3,111	5,143	10,286
Profit after tax	4,236	9,551	19,102
Proposed dividend	1,200	3,600	3,600
Retained profit	3,036	5,951	15,502
Interest cover	2	3	5

Each company has a share capital of £60,000 and a bank loan of £80,000 repayable by 20 equal annual instalments. Ideally, they would all like to pay a dividend of 6 per cent to shareholders. As sales are expected to grow by 10 per cent next year each company wishes to have 8 per cent of this amount available to fund growth in the operating cycle. The profit required is:

Company A £2,921, Company B £1,959 and Company C £4,665.

Table 5.5 shows how the companies are placed to service the constituencies that are interested in their profits.

Table 5.5 The Adequacy of Interest Cover

Company	A	B	C
Interest	7,347	7,347	7,347
Tax	3,111	5,143	10,286
Loan repaid	4,000	4,000	4,000
Dividend required	3,600	3,600	3,600
Growth	2,921	1,959	4,665
PBIT required	20,979	22,049	29,898
Surplus/ (shortfall)	(6,285)	(8)	6,837
PBIT achieved	14,694	22,041	36,735

Company A is poorly placed to fund its expansion. It should not propose the level of dividend that shareholders expect. Even with a reduced dividend, the funds required to contribute towards growth are not sufficient. Company B is well placed to serve all its constituencies. It can grow by 10 per cent and keep gearing under control. Company C is very well placed. It has enough funds to allow a growth rate of 24.7 per cent and, if it will not grow at this pace, it can increase the dividend. This type of analysis has led bankers to believe that a cover of three times the interest cost is needed to service properly the constituencies that are interested in profit. A business is obliged to pay interest and tax and to make loan repayments. Consequently, a shortage of profit before interest and tax (PBIT) should result in a reduced dividend or a restriction on the pace of growth. Even though the main preoccupation of the bank is to collect its interest and loan repayments, it will be watching the planned and actual interest cover to see whether the customer can service all the constituencies adequately.

CAPITALISED INTEREST

When measuring interest cover, you can sometimes come across a problem. When a company buys a new building, the price it pays includes interest on the money borrowed by the developer to construct it. A company, not in the construction industry, might choose to develop a site itself. It seems reasonable in these circumstances to add the interest on the money borrowed to buy the land and to develop it to the cost of the asset created. To do so takes the interest out of the profit and loss account and allows the real cost of the asset to be reported. This treatment, often adopted by hotels, is very satisfactory. However, it distorts the interest cover test.

	Correct Analysis	**Incorrect Analysis**
Profit before interest	20,164	20,164
Interest	8,066	2,066
Cover	2.5	9.76

£6,000 of interest was capitalised. It will still have to be paid and profits are the only source of funds available to pay it.

SUMMARY

A company should have a regular financial electrocardiograph. This is done by measuring gearing and interest cover. If the gearing is too high, or the interest cover is too low, a business has serious problems.

Gearing is the relationship between funds supplied by the owners of a business and those supplied by bankers. The lower the gearing, the more secure the bank is. The higher the gearing, the greater the risk to which a bank is exposed. The wise organisation will draw up a predicted future balance sheet before embarking on a major expansion programme. If the ensuing gearing is too high, the choice is between obtaining more shareholders' funds and restricting the scale of growth. Profit before interest is required for five purposes.

1. To pay the interest.
2. To make loan repayments when they fall due.
3. To pay the tax on the profits of the business.
4. To pay dividends to shareholders.
5. To contribute towards growth in assets as the business expands.

If the interest cover is less than 3, then the funds available to contribute towards business expansion will not be adequate. Failure to maintain adequate gearing and interest cover puts a business at risk. At best, it will result in suggestions by the bankers to dispose of assets in order to restore gearing to a safe level. At worst, it can precipitate a receivership, administration or liquidation.

CHAPTER 6

FOLLOW THE BEST ACCOUNTING PRACTICE: THE PULSE TEST

Financial results are influenced by decisions of the directors on how to fairly record and report complex transactions. For example, the directors must decide on the depreciation policy. The trouble is that a small minority of managers choose to misrepresent financial results. They do this by reporting complex transactions in misleading ways. As part of their corporate governance responsibilities, directors should choose accounting policies that will lead their company towards financial rectitude and not jail.

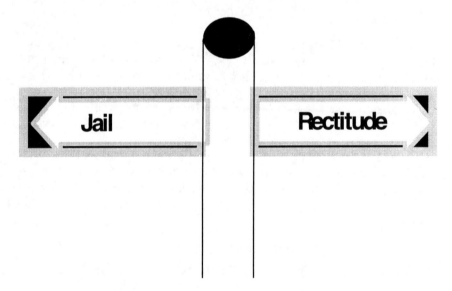

Joan Green started Greenwear two years ago. Her company makes environmentally friendly ladies clothes. The first year of operations was a difficult struggle. One of her major problems was her unit labour cost. It was much higher than those of competitors from the Far East. Early in its second year she landed a three-year contract to supply 20,000 garments per month to a UK multiple. Armed with this major prop, the business thrived. In her second year of trading, Greenwear earned a profit of £55,135 after tax.

After completion of the accounts, for the second year, her auditor told

Joan that he valued the business at in excess of £0.5 million. The trade union, of which most staff were members, asked her for sight of the audited accounts, as part of the negotiation on a new wage agreement. Joan handed over the accounts with considerable pride. Three days later the shop steward landed a claim for a 20 per cent increase on her desk. Joan was aghast. She knew that her unit wage cost would be more than four times as high as her Far Eastern competitor, if she accepted the claim. She also knew that she would lose money on each of the 640,000 garments still to be supplied to the UK multiple.

Joan argued that the business could not afford the wage demand. She said she was prepared to offer a 3 per cent increase. This would more than exceed the rise in the cost of living. She would not offer one penny more. The shop steward argued that Greenwear had earned excessive profits, at the expense of its staff, and stated that the only viable alternative to the increase demanded was a retrospective profit sharing scheme. This would give 40 per cent of the annual profit before tax to the unionised employees. Joan regretted the fact that she had given a copy of the accounts to the trade union. She also regretted the fact that the profits were so high. To grant the retrospective profit share would cost the business in excess of £25,000 for last year alone. She even wondered whether it would have been possible to report a significantly lower profit had she foreseen the demand for a profit share.

Joan had learnt a tough lesson. She had learned that the various stakeholders might be looking for different things when they read a set of accounts. If Joan had decided that the primary purpose of the accounts was to depress an unreasonable demand for a wage increase or a profit share, then she could, quite legitimately, have done things to reduce the published profit. Whether this would have been a prudent action is debatable. Lower profits might have damaged her relationship with other stakeholders. While controlling a business Joan, or any other proprietor, must recognise that the accounting policies used, and the financial results that emerge as a result, may be used to advance their own interests.

Figure 6.1: The Stakeholder Model

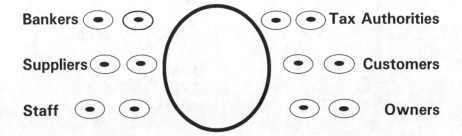

Bankers are most interested in how safe the business is. Suppliers should be even more attuned to this. They usually rank as unsecured creditors. Staff are most interested in profits. Indeed some cynics describe profits as undistributed wages. The tax authorities are interested in taxable profits. Customers are usually most interested in the ability of their supplier to develop the products and services that they will wish to buy in the future. The owners are most interested in the dividends that will be paid to them and the shareholder value created on their behalf. The trouble is that some stakeholders are interested in profitability, whereas others are interested in financial stability. Indeed, some stakeholders want to see high profits and others want to see low ones.

A major challenge facing a business manager is to strike a balance in financial reporting that keeps all stakeholders reasonably happy. They must do this within the constraints of accounting standards and business ethics. A core issue in reporting business performance is that accounting is meant to be conservative. The foundations for correct accounting are based on three key principles.

1. You should make provision for all known losses.

2. You should not anticipate profits until they are earned.

3. Once you set an accounting policy, you should follow it consistently.

THE PULSE TEST

Taking the pulse of an organisation as an approach to financial recording and reporting is like the lie detector test used in criminal investigations. The problem is that it is possible to present data in an optimistic or pessimistic light, or somewhere in between.

Figure 6.2: Approaches to Financial Recording

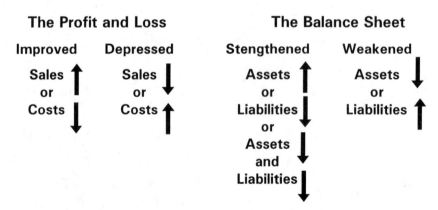

Why might a business wish to depress sales? The local subsidiary of a major multinational knew that the parent business demanded a 20 per cent increase in profits from its operating companies each year. The greater the profit that the local company earned, the higher the platform would be upon which the 20 per cent increase was demanded. To counteract this extrapolation, the local operating company used to date all supplies to customers, after the parent target had been exceeded, into the following year. Another company, quoted on a stock market, invoiced a software product that did not work with a view to shoring up profits in a disastrous year. Actions such as these are a poor reflection on the management of the companies concerned. Nevertheless, they pinpoint potential 'soft spots' in accounting. Even the simple accounting term sales is open to optimistic and pessimistic interpretations.

Have you noticed that when a business falls on hard times the results tend to be far worse than you might have expected? There is usually a simple explanation. In boom times many businesses tend to take a more optimistic view of certain transactions than they should. When business is depressed they often decide to remove all optimistic 'skeletons' from the closet. Issues that surface are:

- stock valuation;
- bad debt provisions;
- customer credit notes;
- rationalisation provisions.

How to flatter the Profit and Loss Account

If the key priority is to maximise profits, then the major challenge is to legitimately find ways to minimise cost. The areas to address are as follows.

1. **Depreciation policy.** The longer the life attributed to a tangible fixed asset, the lower will be the depreciation charge that hits the profit and loss account. Consider motor vehicles.

	Conservative	Optimistic
Cost	18,000	18,000
Life	4 years	6 years
Policy	Straight line	Straight line
Annual charge	£4,500	£3,000

To adopt a six-year life will add £1,500 to the profits as compared to using a four-year life. However, a decision to use a conservative or optimistic life will have no impact on the corporation tax liability. The Inland Revenue disallows depreciation as a cost in determining taxable profits. They give a standard wear and tear allowance in its place.

2. **Stock valuation.**   In Chapter 1 we saw that stock was charged against profit in the month it was sold not the month in which it was bought or made. As a result we can conclude that the higher the value of stock, the lower will be the cost of sales and the higher the profit. There is a narrow line between correctly valuing stock on an optimistic basis and overstating the value of stock. The latter is fraudulent and is something that auditors search for. An excessive valuation will lead to an overstatement of both assets and profits. If discovered it will lead to a qualification of the 'true and fair view' certificate.

3. **Treatment of goodwill.**   In Chapter 5 we saw that goodwill could be carried as an asset or cancelled against reserves. If goodwill is carried as an asset it will be deemed to have a finite, but difficult to measure, life. Companies that decide to treat goodwill as an asset often apply a life of twenty years. One-twentieth is deducted from the asset value and charged as depreciation in each year. To apply a life of five or ten years would increase the charge in the profit and loss account, and result in a lower reported profit and a smaller asset value.

4. **Valuation of trade debtors.**   The value of trade debtors depends on the ability of the seller to collect them. When preparing financial statements, it is necessary to make judgements about which amounts are not likely to be collected and to remove such amounts from the balance sheet. This is done by charging them as bad debts in the profit and loss account. In addition to eliminating bad debts, some consideration should be given to making a provision for debts that currently appear collectable but might turn bad in the future. Even 'blue chip' businesses have failed in recent years. A wise organisation will make a general provision against the debts that could become uncollectable in the future. Such a provision is not mandatory. Consider the impact on profit of an optimistic and pessimistic valuation of trade debtors.

	Optimistic	Pessimistic
Book value of good debts	£145,550	£145,550
Provision %	—	2
Charge against profits	—	£2,911
Balance sheet value	£145,550	£142,639

The tax liability of the business will not be affected by the decision to include, or exclude, a provision for possible future bad debts. Unlike the write-off of specific debts, such charges against profits, are disallowed by the Inland Revenue.

5. **Capitalisation of interest.**   As we saw in Chapter 5 it is sometimes legitimate to include interest on the cost of creating your own asset in the

balance sheet valuation. To do so removes the cost from the profit and loss account and adds to the profit of the business.

6. **Product and market development.** It may be difficult to decide when certain costs associated with developing new products and markets should be charged against profits. A simple example is a payment on account for work done to develop a new advertising campaign that had not started at the end of a financial year. Should the cost be charged against income in that year or treated as a prepayment? To treat the costs as a prepayment can certainly be justified. Costs involved in developing new products are more difficult to handle. SSAP13 rules that expenditure on pure research should be written off in the year in which it is incurred. Expenditure on development can be deferred to future periods if:
    (a) there is a clearly defined project;
    (b) the related expenditure is separately identifiable;
    (c) the outcome of the project has been assessed with reasonable certainty as to its technical feasibility and commercial viability;
    (d) the aggregate of the deferred development costs, any further development costs, and related production, selling and administration costs is reasonably expected to be exceeded by related future sales or other revenues;
    (e) adequate resources exist, or are reasonably expected to be available, to enable the project to be completed and to provide any consequential increases in working capital.

7. **Foreign currency translations.** If a business has a subsidiary, whose books are maintained in a foreign currency, the results must be translated into local currency for inclusion in the accounts. SSAP20 permits the translation of sales and costs to be done at either the rate ruling at the end of the reporting period (closing rate) or the average rate through the period. If the local currency strengthened through the reporting period, then average rate will reveal a higher profit than closing rate (see Table 6.1). If the local currency weakened through the reporting period, then closing rate translation will reveal a higher profit than average rate (see Table 6.2).

Table 6.1: Local Currency Strengthens

	FX	Average Rate		Closing Rate	
	FX	Rate	Translation	Rate	Translation
Sales	105,643	£ = FX1.50	70,429	£ = FX1.60	66,027
Costs	87,394		58,263		54,621
Profit	18,249		12,166		11,406

Average rate shows the higher profit.

Table 6.2: Local Currency Weakens

		Average Rate		Closing Rate	
	FX	Rate	Translation	Rate	Translation
Sales	135,642	£ = FX 1.40	96,887	£ = FX1.30	104,340
Costs	119,115		85,082		91,627
Profits	16,527		11,805		12,713

Closing rate translation shows the higher profit.

Choice of average or closing rate affects the profit and loss account. It is totally different from the treatment of foreign currency sales and purchases and the exchange risk management issues that are dealt with in Chapter 7.

All of these issues have an effect on the profit that a business can report. The directors must decide how each factor should be treated within the constraints of accounting rules. Failure to do so leaves important policy decisions to the auditors by default. In the era of corporate governance, the directors will be responsible for the policy issues whether they formulated them or not.

The principles of accounting require consistent application of policies once formulated. Any change in policy that has a significant impact on the reported profit will result in a qualification of the auditor's report.

How to flatter the Balance Sheet

As was the case with the profit and loss account, it is possible to present a balance sheet in a more or less favourable light. The general principle is that the higher the assets, or the lower the liabilities, the stronger will be the balance sheet. Furthermore, actions to minimise costs will result in higher assets, whereas actions to minimise or eliminate assets will result in higher costs. If you wish to make your assets as strong as possible, you can:

(a) take an optimistic view of the value of stocks and debtors;

(b) set the longest credible lives for tangible fixed assets;

(c) carry goodwill as an asset rather than cancelling it against reserves;

(d) capitalise interest on fixed assets you make for yourself;

(e) defer the cost of development expenditure;

(f) include brands in the balance sheet as a separate and valuable asset. If you do this the brand value must be depreciated through the profit and loss account. Consequently, brand valuation strengthens the balance sheet while weakening the profit and loss account;

(g) revalue appreciating assets, such as land and buildings.

Strangely, a higher asset value can either strengthen or weaken financial stability. For example, if you make an upward revaluation of fixed assets, the increase is recorded in revaluation reserve and strengthens the shareholders' funds. Buying extra stock weakens the balance sheet because it adds to the liabilities as well as the assets. Sometimes to show a high value for assets leads to a balance sheet that appears weaker than is necessary. There are two particularly important issues.

1. To prepare a balance sheet at a high season point will reveal high stocks and debtors and consequently high creditors and overdrafts. It is wise to have your accounting year end in the low season.

2. Proprietors whose principal goal is to sell the business often postpone the replacement of fixed assets. This minimises:
    *   gearing;
    *   depreciation;
    *   interest charges.

Where fixed assets have been allowed to run down, an astute bidder will realise that a successful acquisition will have to be followed by heavy capital expenditure, to restore cost competitiveness, and will limit the size of the offer to reflect this.

How to reduce Profits

As we saw earlier in this chapter, Joan Green might have been interested in reducing her profit to relieve pressure for a wage increase or profit share. To do this Joan would have to adopt accounting policies designed to increase costs and reduce assets. She might:

(a) set the shortest possible life for fixed assets;

(b) provide for obsolete stock and potentially doubtful debts;

(c) carry goodwill or brands as an asset and depreciate them;

(d) avoid capitalising product development costs or interest.

The material in this chapter is designed to help you set appropriate accounting policies, and to recognise the effect that such policies have on financial performance. Fraudulent attempts, by a tiny minority of black sheep, to inflate sales and assets or suppress costs and liabilities have no place in this book, and I deplore them. Equally, the attention of the Accounting Standards Board is firmly fixed on the 'financial engineers' who spend their time looking for loopholes in accounting legislation that will enable them to show financial results in an unduly flattering light.

SUMMARY

Financial and management accounts help you to keep your finger on the pulse of your organisation. There is scope, within the constraints of lawful accounting, to paint the financial picture of a business in a variety of ways. The owners and directors must select accounting policies that will paint an appropriate picture for all stakeholders. The results can be significantly influenced by the accounting policies chosen. Various stakeholders want different things from financial reports. The proprietors must decide whether the priority is to:

(a) take the pressure off demands for excessive wage increases;

(b) pay as little tax as possible;

(c) reassure your bankers and suppliers;

(d) discourage an unwanted takeover bid;

(e) have some other primary reporting priority.

CHAPTER 7

CLEANED OUT BY A STRONG CURRENCY: ANTI-EMETICS

The best businesses have recognised that the world is their marketplace. They are prepared to buy or sell in any currency in spite of the risks involved. This meets the needs of suppliers and customers who will only trade if transactions are denominated in their local currency. When transactions are denominated in foreign currencies, there is an additional risk of losses as a result of unfavourable exchange rate movements. The losses can occur by making purchases or sales in foreign currencies. They can also occur by having assets or liabilities in foreign currencies. The biggest problems occur when a business buys or sells on credit. Consider Table 7.1.

Table 7.1: Selling when your Local Currency Strengthens

Sales	Exchange Rate at sale	Exchange Rate at settlement	Loss
FX312,000	£1 = FX1.20	£1 = FX1.30	20,000

In Table 7.1 you hope to receive £260,000. You receive £240,000. Exporters fear local currency strength. Sterling proceeds fall as that currency appreciates. An exporter is faced with 'Hobson's choice'. If prices are increased, then volume will fall, if prices are not increased, then margin will fall.

Table 7.2: Buying when your Local Currency Weakens

Purchases	Exchange Rate at purchase	Exchange Rate at settlement	Loss
FX280,000	£ = FX80	£ = FX70	500

In Table 7.2 importers expect to pay £3,500. You pay £4,000. Importers fear currency weakness. Sterling cost rises as that currency depreciates. Importers may not be able to recover the extra costs through higher selling prices.

Exchange rates are volatile and unpredictable. Nobody can tell whether a currency will strengthen or weaken in the future. They simply analyse the factors that help and hinder a currency at the moment and try to extrapolate them into the future. Their predictions for future exchange rates are wrong as often as they are right.

Table 7.3: Selling when your Local Currency Weakens

Sales	Exchange rate at sale	Exchange rate at settlement	Gain
FX 312,000	£1 = FX1.30	£1 = FX1.20	20,000

In Table 7.3 you hope to receive £240,000. You receive £260,000. Exporters love local currency weakness. Sterling proceeds rise as that currency depreciates.

Table 7.4: Buying when your Local Currency Strengthens

Purchases	Exchange rate at purchase	Exchange rate at settlement	Gain
FX280,000	£ = FX70	£ = FX80	500

In Table 7.4 you expect to pay £4,000. You pay £3,500. Importers love local currency strength. Sterling costs fall as that currrency appreciates.

It is certainly nice when an exchange rate moves in your favour and provides you with an extra benefit (higher receipts or lower costs) However, to gamble on this can leave your business exposed to unacceptable losses if the exchange rate moves in the wrong direction.

The wise business will recognise that gambling is not part of their mission, and will take steps to eliminate the potential for currency losses, often sacrificing the potential for gains in order to achieve this end. The Barings Bank debacle is one of many examples of unwarranted speculation, in which a gambler lost an organisation its shirt. This should be a salutary lesson for even quite small businesses. The lesson is that currency speculation can make your business sick. Fortunately there are six anti-emetics available to you.

You can:

1. *Refuse to do business in a foreign currency*. This ostrich like approach can result in you failing to achieve profitable sales or competitive costs. I do not recommend it.

2. *Arrange to have an equal amount of purchases and sales in the foreign currency*. In this way any losses on sales will be cancelled by gains on purchases or vice versa. A small problem with this approach is that it costs money to process transactions in foreign currencies.

3. *Have a bank account in the foreign country denominated in the currency of that country*. This overcomes the transaction cost problem that I mentioned in method two. However, it is still necessary to have an equal value of purchases and sales. Failure to do this leaves your business exposed to translation losses on the foreign bank account when the asset or liability is converted on paper into your local currency for balance sheet purposes.

4. *Arrange a forward rate agreement*. This currency risk technique is possible because sellers fear local currency strength and buyers fear local currency weakness. Forward rate agreements are explained later in this chapter.

5. *Arrange a foreign currency option contract*. This is based on fears of

appreciation and depreciation. Options are explained later in this chapter.

6. *Have equal amounts of assets and liabilities denominated in a foreign currency.*

John Brush runs a small export business. Last year he made a worthwhile profit. This year has been difficult due to the strength of sterling. For example, compare his results for June of last year and this year.

	Last year	This year
Sales	45,743	36,503
Cost of sales	34,307	34,972
Gross margin	11,436	1,531
Overheads	6,693	6,794
Profit (loss)	4,743	(5,263)

You may be surprised to learn that the quantity John sold was 5 per cent higher in June of this year than in June of last year. The reason for the loss was that John billed his customers in their currency. Sterling had strengthened dramatically, through the previous year. This wreaked havoc on the value of his sales.

	Last year	This year
Billed to customers	43,456	45,629
Sterling equivalent	45,743	36,503
Average exchange rate achieved	£1 = FX0.95	£1 = FX1.25

Sterling strength ruined the effect of a higher volume. John was caught up in a problem that faces any exporter when his local currency strengthens. The same problem arises for importers when their local currency weakens.

John was in a difficult position. He would have to increase his selling prices by 27.1 per cent and sell the same quantities in order to earn the same gross margin as he had earned in the previous June. John knew that an increase in prices of this size would wipe out the demand for his products. He saw little opportunity to reduce his costs and felt that the prospects for his small, but previously thriving, business were dismal. Like many businesses John failed to diagnose and manage his currency risk. He was gambling that his local currency would remain stable or weaken without even realising it. John might have been able to avoid the sickness had he been aware that antiemetics, described earlier in the chapter, were available.

Some businesses find it impractical to arrange equal amounts of purchases and sales in a foreign currency. If they still wish to trade overseas, they should consider forward rate agreements or option contracts. Each of these ways to eliminate exchange losses is based on the fact that a bank must balance its books. For example, when a bank buys dollars from you it must sell them to someone else. The counterparty can be either a local business that wishes to buy the dollars to pay a US supplier, or a US business that wishes to convert the proceeds of their foreign currency sale into dollars. Table 7.5 explains the two-legged transactions.

Table 7.5: The Two Sides of Foreign Currency Purchases and Sales

Action	Consequence 1	Consequence 2
1. Local company sells in dollars	Sell dollars	Buy local
2. Local company buys in dollars	Buy dollars	Sell local
3. US company sells in local	Sell local	Buy dollars
4. US company buys in local	Buy local	Sell dollars

In Table 7.5 the matching actions are:

(a) 1 with 2 or 3;

(b) 2 with 1 or 4;

(c) 3 with 1 or 4;

(d) 4 with 2 or 3.

In a situation where a bank has a higher value of offers to sell dollars than to buy them, it will increase the exchange rate to discourage dollar sales and encourage dollar purchases. Equally, in a situation where a bank has a lower value of offers to sell dollars than to buy them, it will decrease the exchange rate to encourage dollar sales and discourage dollar purchases.

When arranging to sell foreign currency on the spot (today's) market, the bank will quote a rate, such as £ = $1.47–1.50. If you are selling $495,000, you will receive £330,000 (495,000 / 1.50). If you are buying $485,100, you will pay £330,000 (485,100 / 1.47). The bank buys high (the right-hand quotation) but it sells low (the left-hand quotation). When a business makes foreign currency purchases the cost rises as the local currency weakens. If an equal value of imports are made the revenue will rise and cancel out the cost deficit (see Table 7.6).

Table 7.6: Imports can Cancel Cost Deficit

		Transaction		Settlement	
	Value FX	**Rate**	**Reported**	**Rate**	**Reported**
Purchases	485,100	£ = FX1.47	330,000	£ = FX1.323	366,667
Sales	495,000	£ = FX1.50	330,000	£ = FX1.35	366,667

Deficit on purchases £36,667. Surplus on sales £36,667.

Figure 7.1: Relationship Between Foreign Exchange Rates and Foreign Sales

	Strong	**Weak**
Imports	Costs fall	Costs rise
Exports	Proceeds fall	Proceeds rise

FORWARD SALE AGREEMENTS

Forward sale agreements are based on the matching of equal and opposite exposures. A core question that a business, which buys or sells in foreign currencies, must ask itself is whether it is prepared to forgo the possibility of exchange rate gains in return for the elimination of the risk of exchange rate losses. If it is prepared to accept this trade-off, then forward sale agreements can be used.

You sold goods worth $400,000 to a customer in the USA at a time when the exchange rate was £ = $1.50. This amount is due for payment in three months' time. You could gamble that the exchange rate would:

(a) remain stable, in which case you will receive £266,667;

(b) weaken to say £ = $1.40, in which case you will receive £285,714. The snag is that it could strengthen to say £ = $1.60 in which case you will only receive £250,000. Is the chance that a 10 cent change in exchange rates could add £19,047, or subtract £16,667, worth taking? In a small business the latter exchange rate could wipe out its profit and is a foolish gamble. If you talked to the treasury department in your bank they might offer you a guarantee of £267,981 in three months' time. They can do this because your fear of damage to your revenue from sterling strength can be matched against that of a US company that is buying goods or services in the UK and also fears sterling strength. If the bank can match these equal and opposite exposures, nobody loses but equally nobody gains. This form of insurance is totally justified since the objective of

Seller

Banker

Buyer

most businesses is to sell goods and services not to speculate in currencies.

The principle behind this swap is that the seller, fearing local currency strength, will forgo the possibility of receiving more than £267,981 in order to guarantee that they will not receive less than this amount. Equally, the buyer, fearing local currency weakness, will forgo the possibility that it will cost less than £267,981 in order to guarantee that it will not cost more.

The Mechanics of a Forward Sale Agreement

Assumptions

1. An English company sells goods, valued at $400,000 to a customer in the USA. It expects to be paid in three months' time,

2. Inter-bank interest rates are: London 8 per cent per annum and New York 6 per cent per annum.

3. Current exchange rate is £1 = $1.50

Step 1: Borrow $394,089 in New York. You will use the proceeds from the customer to repay the loan plus the $5,911 of interest that will accrue over the next three months. The amount to be borrowed is calculated by dividing $400,000 by 1.015. This removes 1.5 per cent interest and pinpoints the amount of borrowings needed.

Borrow $400,000 / 1.015	$394,089
Interest charged $394,089 at 6 per cent p.a. for three months	5,911
Repaid from customer collection	$400,000

Step 2: You convert the amount borrowed into sterling. The £262,726 you receive is calculated as $394,089 divided by 1.5. It is deposited in a bank in London. It earns interest of £5,255. In three months' time your deposit account will total £267,981.

Deposit $394,089 / 1.5	£262,726
Interest earned £267,981 at 2 per cent p.a. for three months	5,255
Amount collected	£267,981

The £267,981 cannot be affected by exchange rate movements over the next three months. It simply reflects the spot exchange rate of £ = $1.50 and the fact that inter-bank rates are slightly higher in London than in New York. Note that to compensate you for the greater interest rate on deposits, you will receive £1,314 more than if you had been able to make the sale for immediate cash.

Interest earned	£5,255
Interest paid $5,911 / 1.5	£3,941
Net gain	£1,314

The dollars are sold at the forward exchange rate ruling on the day when the forward contract is arranged. This is £ = $1.4926 ($400,000 / £267,981). Do you think the forward sale agreement is more attractive than running the risk of sterling strength?

The calculations above are used to work out a forward sale agreement. The creation of loan and deposit accounts is not necessary as the bank will arrange to match a business that wishes to sell dollars against one that wishes to buy dollars. This matching of equal and opposite exposures eliminates the risk of losses for both parties.

The Mechanics of a Forward Purchase Agreement

Assumptions

1. An English company buy goods from a supplier in the USA. They expect to pay US$400,000 in three months' time,

2. Inter-bank interest rates are: London 8 per cent per annum and New York 6 per cent per annum.

3. Current exchange rate is £1 = $1.50.

Step 1: Borrow £262,726 in London. You will be charged interest at 8 per cent per annum for three months. The amount to be borrowed is determined by the need to create a deposit account of $394,089 in New York. This is £262,726 multiplied by 1.5.

You will have to repay £267,981. When you repay this amount in three months' time it will cost £1,314 more than if you bought the goods for cash.

Borrow $394,089 / 1.5	£262,726
Interest paid £262,726 at 8 per cent p.a. for three months	5,255
Amount to be repaid	£267,981

Step 2: You convert the borrowings to $394,089 and deposit this sum in New York where it earns interest of $5,911. In three months' time your deposit account will total $400,000 and you will use this sum to pay the US supplier.

Deposited	$394,089
Interest earned $394,089 at 6 per cent p.a. for three months	5,911
Available to pay supplier	$400,000

The forward purchase agreement guarantees the cost. The actual cost will be slightly higher than if the purchase was settled on the spot market. This is

because you will pay a higher rate of interest on your London borrowings than you receive on your New York deposit.

Interest earned $5,911 / 1.5	£3,941
Interest paid	£<u>5,255</u>
Net excess cost	£<u>1,314</u>

The forward sale and purchase agreements are mirror images of one another. The bank arranges the marriage of equal and opposite risks. There is no need to create deposit and loan accounts for either party.

FOREIGN CURRENCY OPTION CONTRACTS

Forward sale agreements offer protection against possible loss. They do so at the expense of potential gains. Clearly, an exporter would find it much nicer if it could take any gains that would arise through currency weakness, but avoid the possibility of loss through currency strength. Option contracts enable you to do this, but at a cost. In law, the word 'option' gives you a right to take a certain action if circumstances favour doing so, but does not impose an obligation to take this action if circumstances are unfavourable.

Option to Sell ('put')

Consider our previous example of a sale valued at $400,000 and a current exchange rate of £=$1.50. If you were offered an option to sell dollars at this rate would you consider it attractive? It would allow you to exercise ('put') the option if sterling strengthened and avoid loss while leaving you the opportunity to refuse the option and gain from any sterling weakness. This is like a wonderful game of coin tossing where the rules are heads you win and tails you don't lose. Consider the outcome at various exchange rates in Table 7.7.

Table 7.7: Exercising the Put Option at Various Exchange Rates

	Case 1	Case 2	Case 3	Case 4
Rate	£=$1.30	£=$1.40	£=$1.60	£=$1.70
Proceeds if exercised	£266,667	£266,667	£266.667	£266.667
Proceeds if selling spot	£307,692	£285,714	£250,000	£235,294
Loss if exercising	£41,025	£19,047		
Gain from exercising			£16,667	£31,373
Should you exercise?	No	No	Yes	Yes

The only snag is that there is an entry fee for the game. It would cost about £5,000 to arrange this sell ('put') option. This cost is paid up front. As a result, if the option is not exercised your net collection will be £261,667 rather than £266,667. If the exchange rate is more than £=$1.50 it will be profitable to exercise the option. The most attractive feature of a 'put' option is that it enables the holder to create a playing pitch that is level with those that gamble on currency weakness while avoiding the potential loss associated with currency strength.

Option to Buy ('Call')

When a business is buying goods or services priced in a foreign currency, it will fear currency weakness. This would push the price up. Suppose a UK company buys goods at a cost of $400,000 when the exchange rate is £=S1.50. If you were offered an option to buy dollars at this rate would you consider it attractive? It would allow you to exercise ('call') the option if sterling weakened and avoid loss while letting you refuse the option and gain from any sterling strength. Heads you win and tails you don't lose again. Consider the outcome at various exchange rates.

Figure 7.8: Exercising the Call Option at Various Exchange Rates

	Case 1	Case 2	Case 3	Case 4
	£=$1.30	£=$1.40	£=$1.60	£=$1.70
Rate				
Cost if exercised	£266,667	£266,667	£266.667	£266.667
Cost if buying spot	£307,692	£285,714	£250,000	£235,294
Gain from exercising	£41,025	£19,047		
Loss if exercised			£16,667	£31,373
Should you exercise?	Yes	Yes	No	No

It would cost about £5,000 to arrange this buy ('call') option. This cost is paid up front. As a result if the option is not exercised your net cost will be £271,667 rather than £266,667. If the exchange rate is less than £=$1.50 it will be profitable to exercise the option. A buy ('call') option allows the holder to create a playing pitch that is level with those that gamble on currency strength while avoiding the potential loss associated with currency weakness.

Options are based on the principle of swapping the risk of unfavourable exchange rate movements with an appropriate counterparty. The principle is the same as with spot transactions. The match must be between a party that will exercise an option to sell dollars against one that will exercise an option to buy dollars. This party will be a US company whose imports are priced in sterling.

Cover, Don't Gamble

Forward rate agreements and option contracts help an organisation to protect its margins against unfavourable currency movements. They are valuable prescriptions. It is possible to abuse these instruments as many imprudent organisations have found to their cost. The wise organisation will only use them to support real purchase or sale transactions. One of the key monthly reports in an organisation that imports or exports should be a statement of foreign exchange exposures, such as Table 7.9.

Table 7.9: Statement of Foreign Exchange Exposures

Revenue Exposures

Currency	Two-way trade	Forward	Option	Uncovered	Total
DM	347,000	—	800,000	127,953	1,274,953
FF	456,350	675,000	—	124,987	1,256,337

Cost Exposures

Currency	Two-way trade	Forward	Option	Uncovered	Total
DM	347,000	—	—	—	347,000
FF	456,350	—	—	—	456,350
SF	—	—	1,000,000	125,683	1,125,683

The above table shows the management of exposure for future cash receipts in Germany and France, and the management of exposure for future cash costs in Switzerland. Given the size of the debtor and creditor balances, the uncovered amounts are reasonable.

Arranging Foreign Exchange Transactions and Instruments

The rates that banks offer are based on supply and demand for currencies. For this reason you should get at least two quotations. For example, one bank might quote £ = $1.49-1.51 while another bank might quote £ = $1.48-1.50. If you were buying $500,000 you would accept the first bank quote of £ = $1.49. If you were selling $500,000 you would accept the second bank quote of £ = $1.50.

	Bank 1	Bank 2
Sell for	331,126	333,333 Bank 2 is best
Buy for	335,570	337,838 Bank 1 is best

The experts also recommend that, when you ask for a quotation, you should not specify whether you are buying or selling. This helps to ensure a competitive quotation.

Assets and Liabilities in Foreign Currencies

If your business has assets denominated in a foreign currency, they will have to be translated into local currency for inclusion in your balance sheet. The translation is done at the rate ruling on the balance sheet date. A paper profit or loss can occur on translation. For example, a UK company owned a factory in New York, which cost $210,000. At the date of the previous balance sheet the exchange rate was £=$1.40. The building was incorporated in the balance sheet at £150,000. Twelve months later the exchange rate was £=$1.50. The building would have to be included at a value of £140,000. Even though the building had the same dollar value it would have to be reported at a £10,000 lower sterling value. It is certainly true that if sterling weakened back to £=$1.50 in the following year the loss would be recovered. Nevertheless, the paper loss will have to be deducted from the shareholders' funds and this will drive up the gearing. The strength of sterling is the cause of the paper loss. If sterling had weakened, the UK company would have earned a paper profit.

Another UK business borrowed $210,000 in New York because they found that US interest rates were attractive. At the date of the previous balance sheet the exchange rate was £=$1.50 and the loan was included in their balance sheet at a value of £140,000. At the end of the following year, sterling had weakened to an exchange rate of £=$1.40. The loan was translated into sterling at this rate and included in the balance sheet at £150,000. A paper loss had been incurred as a result of sterling weakness.

It was possible for both businesses to avoid the paper losses. The first company should have borrowed $210,000 in New York. When this loan was translated into sterling for balance sheet inclusion the debt would have fallen to £140,000 as compared with £150,000 in the previous year. The paper loss that occurred as a result of holding a dollar asset would be cancelled against the paper profit from holding a dollar liability as sterling strengthened.

The mistake that the second company made was to repatriate their dollar loan. If it had been invested in dollar assets, the paper loss on translation of the loan as sterling weakened would have been cancelled out by the paper gain on the dollar asset.

These examples should lead you to the conclusion that it is only wise to invest abroad when you have matching borrowings. Equally, it is only wise to borrow abroad when you will invest in matching overseas assets or the expectation of future cash receipts in that currency to cover the loan and interest.

SUMMARY

Most businesses have foreign currency exposures. These relate to purchases, sales, assets and liabilities. In recent years we have seen major movements in exchange rates and these are likely to continue.

1.   The wise organisation will not gamble on stability or favourable movements, since adverse movements will sicken the business.

2.   The cheapest anti-emetic is to source and supply equal amounts in a foreign currency. In this way, any loss on cash receipts will be counterbalanced by a gain on supplier payments or vice versa.

Where this is not possible, treasury management products can eliminate the danger of losses. An organisation can use forward sale agreements or option contracts. As we have seen, the forward sale agreement is less satisfactory. The failure to gain from favourable exchange rate movements can place an organisation in an unsatisfactory competitive position relative to an imprudent uncovered competitor, or one with option contracts. When arranging a foreign currency instrument or transaction make sure to obtain at least two quotations in order to ensure a favourable rate.

   If you buy assets overseas and hold them in foreign currencies, you are exposed to translation losses if sterling strengthens. If you use a similar amount of overseas debt this will cancel the adverse effect of the translation losses. If you repatriate foreign currency borrowings, you leave yourself exposed to translation losses if sterling weakens. Foreign borrowings should only be used to pay for foreign assets. The gain on translation of the assets will cancel the adverse effect of the loss on translation of the debt as sterling weakens.

CHAPTER 8

WHICH PRODUCTS ARE REALLY PROFITABLE?: X-RAYS

Most businesses provide more than one product or service for their customers. In these cases, it is quite possible that some products are very profitable and others are less profitable, or even loss making. The wise manager will try to X-ray the products or services to ascertain which should be promoted and which should be re-engineered. The pictures revealed in the X-rays are a series of smaller product profit and loss accounts that feed into the overall profit of the firm.

Equally, if a business takes a different type of X-ray, it may find that some markets and customers are very profitable whereas others are not. Once again, these pictures provide the data on which important strategic decisions should be made. The wise proprietor will be prepared to have the appropriate product and market profitability analysis carried out as it will provide key information upon which important business decisions will be made.

Tom Frost runs a small supermarket. Not long ago he attended a marketing seminar. One of the things he learned was that he should give the best space to the products that offer the best margins. An extract from a table (Table 8.1) that he asked his bookkeeper to prepare showed his profit margins.

Table 8.1: Sample Profit Margins from Tom Frost's Supermarket

Product	Selling Price	Buying Price	Margin	Margin % Sales
Apples	£12.00	£7.68	£4.32	36%
Tomatoes	£10.00	£6.80	£3.20	32%
Frozen fish	£14.00	£10.36	£3.64	26%
Tobacco	£15.00	£13.50	£1.50	10%

The table confirmed his instinct that fresh fruit and vegetables were the most profitable lines. His previous decision to dedicate his prime selling space to these products had been vindicated. Many frozen foods were high on the table of margins. Tom had not realised that they had the potential to put the icing on his profit cake. He decided to improve the quality of display by introducing new freezer cabinets. They were placed in prime selling space designed to catch the eye of casual shoppers.

Turnover for the next month was much the same as previous periods. Tom noted that sales of frozen foods had increased significantly. He was not concerned that certain other lines, newly deprived of prime selling space, were down. He was confident that the overall profit would have improved significantly. Some time later Tom received a surprisingly large electricity bill. At first he thought it must be a mistake. However, when he checked the meter he found that it was correct. The penny dropped. His new freezers were consuming energy at a frightening rate. He wondered if his margin review and the display changes that he had made as a result were correct. Some time later his quarterly accounts turned out to be very disappointing (see Table 8.2).

Table 8.2: Example of Tom Frost's Quarterly Accounts

	This quarter	Last quarter
Sales	735,955	706,948
Cost of sales	599.787	571,214
Gross margin	136,168	135,734
Staff costs	(68,084)	(67,367)
Overheads	(58,806)	(53,784)
Operating profit	9,278	14,583
Gross margin %	18.50	19.20
Net margin %	1.26	2.06

Major variances

Power	1,369
Maintenance contracts	1,250
Interest	1,344
Depreciation	876
Other	183
	5,022

Tom did not know which products really earned the best margins. Without even realising what he was doing, Tom was using a contribution costing system. This simply challenged his business to make overall sales that were big enough to pay for the suppliers, staff and overheads and to leave him with an adequate profit.

The dynamic business needs to know which products are the winners. It must have a reliable costing system. In Tom's case he unconsciously assumed that the staff costs and other expenses could fairly be attributed to products in proportion to sales. To prove the error of his logic it is only necessary to 'X-ray' three departments.

To obtain accurate product costs you need to break down your budget into material, labour and overhead components, and to find reliable ways to attribute them to products. Until recent years most trading businesses felt that they did not need accurate product costs. The standard approach was to add a mark-up to the supplier price. Since all retailers tended to use the same mark-up nobody gained a competitive advantage. In recent years the competitive stance has changed dramatically. At one end of the scale we have high volume, low price operators, such as discount stores. At the other end of the scale we have low volume high price operators, such as boutiques. The general retailer is being attacked on both flanks. The only satisfactory way to counter these attacks is to adjust your selling prices. This was what led to Tom's discovery that he was obtaining better gross margins from some products than others. His simple buying price, selling price comparison did not tell him the whole story. Correct overhead attribution would have prevented Tom's incorrect assumption about frozen food margins.

Tom needed to establish:

(a) *the total staff cost and the proportions that should be attributed to the various departments*. Much of this work is easy to do. Many staff spend all their time working in one department, such as the butchers, that our careful X-ray disclosed. Some of the staff are more difficult to attribute. For example, Tom had a number of people involved in such diverse tasks as loading the shelves, keeping the shop clean, manning the cash registers, accounting and other administrative jobs. These costs are of a much more general nature. Some shop proprietors may be tempted to attribute them in proportion to sales but this would fail to recognise snags, such as the fact that butchers do their own packing and cleaning and should not be allocated a proportion of the overall packing and cleaning bill as well;

(b) *the total overhead cost and the proportions that should be attributed to the various departments*. As we saw earlier, the overhead costs include substantial technology driven costs related to the frozen foods. A cost allocation system that attributed electricity in proportion to departmental sales would seriously underestimate the real cost of the frozen food section (it would be heavily subsidised) and unfairly load other less machine intensive departments.

Tom should also recognise that other elements of the overhead budget can lead to subsidies to some departments and penalties to others. For example, consider procurement. Purchasing fresh foods from the local markets is much more expensive than ordering 'off-the-shelf' products from local suppliers. If Tom is to prepare reliable costings, he will have to attribute staff and overhead costs accurately. Tom, like any other business manager, needs to use an activity based cost attribution approach.

THE ACTIVITY BASED COST ATTRIBUTION APPROACH

The principles on which an activity based cost attribution system must be built are easy to describe.

Step 1: Prepare an accurate budget for each activity. For example, earlier in this chapter we considered frozen foods. This section of a supermarket will have significant technology costs:

- power;

- maintenance;

- depreciation;

- interest on money borrowed to buy the freezers.

Step 2: Predict the demand for units of the activity. This demand is called the cost driver. For example, Tom should be able to predict the number of kilowatt hours that his freezers will be running.

When Tom divides the cost of the activity by the demand for it, he will obtain the cost per kilowatt hour. The cost for each type of machine will help to clarify the profitability of frozen foods, such as pizzas, vegetables, ice creams, etc. He will use the diagram in Figure 8.1 to attribute other activities.

Figure 8.1: Diagram of ABC

Total activity cost

$$\frac{\blacksquare}{\blacksquare} = \textbf{Cost per unit}$$

Units of activity required

Activity based costing is even more important in manufacturing. An example of the additional problems that you can meet is taken from a maker of men's suits. A significant activity in this business is cutting the cloth. Suppose a customer places an order for 1,000 suits. The make up of the order will be something like Table 8.3.

Table 8.3: Make up of Order for 1,000 Suits

Chest size (inches)	Volume
36	5
38	45
40	225
42	450
44	225
46	45
48	5

Now suppose that we have budgeted the cost of the cutting room activity as £7,200. This suggests a cost per suit of £7.20 but we need to look a little deeper. Suppose that to allow cloths to be cut precisely they should be stacked on top of each other in piles of not more than 45 high. We can now compute a more reliable cutting cost (see Table 8.4).

You Don't Need An Accountant

Table 8.4: Cutting Cost for 1,000 Suits

Size	Cuts	Cost per cut	Total cost	Suits	Cost per suit
36	1	300[1]	300	5	60.00
38	1	300	300	45	6.67
40	5	300	1,500	225	6.67
42	10	300	3,000	450	6.67
44	5	300	1,500	225	6.67
46	1	300	300	45	6.67
48	1	300	300	5	60.00
	24		7,200	1,000	

[1] £7,200 / 24 = £300

This data show us that men buying the extra small and extra large suits, at exactly the same retail price, are being subsidised to the tune of £53.33 by men buying suits in sizes closer to average. It also pinpoints an opportunity for a specialised retailer who offers suits at a lower price but only carries suits in sizes from 38 to 46. Now suppose the retailer wanted a slightly different order (see Table 8.5).

Table 8.5: Variation on order for 1,000 Suits

Chest size (inches)	Volume
36	5
38	50
40	225
42	440
44	225
46	50
48	5

In order to meet this order the company will have to do 26 cuttings. We will suppose the budgeted cost is £7,800. See Table 8.6 for the new cutting cost per suit.

Table 8.6: New Cutting Cost per 1,000 Suits

Size	Cuts	Cost per cut	Total cost	Suits	Cost per suit
36	1	300	300	5	60.00
38	2	300	600	50	12.00
40	5	300	1,500	225	6.67
42	10	300	3,000	440	6.82
44	5	300	1,500	225	6.67
46	2	300	600	50	12.00
48	1	300	300	5	60.00
	26		7,800	1,000	

It should be obvious from this table that the manufacturer would do everything possible to persuade the retailer to buy in the original proportions thus making an additional £600 on the order. There are certainly examples of this kind that you should be able to identify in your business sector.

How to assemble the Costs of an Activity Correctly

In a manufacturing company accurate product costings are essential:

(a) make or buy decisions must be correct;

(b) product promotion decisions must be designed to attract customers to the most profitable mix, etc.

The cost of production in a manufacturing company can be divided into four major components.

Cost Type	Attribution Method
• Material	Book to products on issue from stores.
• Direct labour	Book to products using job cards.
• Facilities	Book to products in proportion to space.
• Technology and services	Book to products as they 'buy' time.

Figures 8.2: Core Costs in Manufacturing

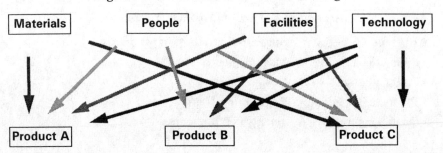

The following example shows you how to predict and attribute facility costs.

Step 1: Predict the cost for the whole factory.

Rent and rates	36,135
Light and heat	11,891
Insurance	7,309
Maintenance buildings	3,521
Depreciation buildings	1,144
Total expenditure	60,000

Step 2: Assess the space of the whole factory (12,000 sq. ft).

Step 3: Divide the £60,000 facility cost by the cost driver (square feet) to obtain a cost per square foot. In this example, it is £5.

Step 4: Assess the square footage devoted to the activity. If it is 1,200 sq. ft, then the space cost to be attributed is £6,000.

The technology cost is computed using a similar approach.

Step 1: Collect the cost for each machine.

Operators' remuneration	18,635
Power	6,945
Insurance	3,136
Maintenance	1,553
Space	6,000 (previous aggregation)
Depreciation	1,731
Total	38,000

Step 2: Assess the expected running hours (50 weeks at 40 hours per week).

Step 3: Compute the cost per hour, £19 in this case.

Step 4: Charge £19 per hour to any product buying time on the machine. Machine hour rates are the ideal way to charge for the use of equipment in a manufacturing business. A printing press is an ideal example.

Examples of Costs that should be Activity Base Attributed

Cost type	Suggested attribution mechanism
• Product machining	Machine hours.
• Product design	Design hours.
• Product engineering	Engineering hours.
• Quality control	Quality control hours.

- Procurement   Number of procurements.
- Packing   Packing hours.
- Shipping   By customer and market.

How to prepare Reliable Product Costs

1. You have to believe that the time you will invest to compute accurate product costs is worth spending. In the competitive world leading to the 21st century, the arguments in favour of this time investment seem to me to be compelling. Customers expect both best cost producers and 'niche' providers to be offering products and services. They demand value as well as quality. They are prepared to pay a high price if there are few producers, and a lower price if there are many. A high price usually means that potential competitors recognise that the activities involved are expensive.

2. You will need carefully prepared and reliable cost budgets. Some businesses prepare the costs for last week, last month or last year. In my view, this is a complete waste of time. You cannot change financial history, whether you like the results or not. If you do not like what the budget for the next period tells you at least you have time to explore a more profitable route into the future.

3. You will need to spread your major costs over the activities that they are incurred to support. To achieve this, you will have to address the activity cost and volume issues raised earlier in this chapter. These create the X-ray eyes that enable you to look deep inside your business and find opportunities for competitive advantage. A computer spreadsheet can help

you keep track of the total planned expenditure to be apportioned through activities to products.

4. Technology costs lend themselves to activity based attribution. This is not true of all costs. For example, the cost of administration is significant in most organisations. I do not think this cost is suitable for activity based attribution. The money is spent for the collective benefit of the organisation and there is no reliable volume measure for use in attribution to products. The costs that fail to offer a satisfactory volume driver can be spread over products in proportion to sales or to direct labour (see Table 8.7).

Table 8.7: Spreading Costs Over Products

Product	A	B	C	D	Total	Attribution Method
Sales	60,000	80,000	50,000	60,000	250,000	
Material	12,000	28,000	18,500	21,500	80,000	Product specific
Procurement	240	580	320	160	1,300	Orders placed
Product labour	27,945	39,635	18,329	23,457	109,366	Standard hours
Design	900	1,850	220	140	3,110	Design hours
Distribution	3,800	8,200	2,000	3,000	17,000	Postal deliveries
Admin.	4,500	6,000	3,750	4,500	18,750	7.5% of sales
Total cost	49,385	84,265	43,119	52,757	229,526	
Profit	10,615	(4,265)	6,881	7,243	20,474	

Product B is clearly a major problem. This would not be recognised if all of the overheads were allocated in proportion to sales. Since it is expected to create the greatest sales value it needs to be addressed immediately. The first thing that should strike you is that it is much more labour intensive than the other products. Is this because Tom's labour force are less efficient than that of his competitors or because the company is selling the product at too low a price? It is vital to discover whether it is these factors or some other reason that causes product B to be unprofitable. Once the true cause is ascertained, it should be possible to tackle the problem.

Customer Profitability is also an Important Strategic Issue

Many businesses are finding that customers are requesting lower prices for large orders. These requests are quite reasonable. Costs per unit decline as the volumes ordered and delivered rise. Simple examples of this include design and delivery. The design cost for a product is usually similar whether

Figures 8.2: Core Costs in Manufacturing

| Materials | People | Facilities | Technology |

| Product A | Product B | Product C |

you hope to make and sell 50 or 500 units. Equally, it should not cost twice as much to deliver 200 units as it would for 100. Suppliers who recognise this will be prepared to reduce the price they charge as the size of order increases. This type of price reduction should not be driven by a simplistic view of economies of scale. The sensible proprietor will prepare a forecast profit and loss account for each large customer.

The attribution approaches described in assessing profitability by product are again followed in customer profitability analysis. Selling price reductions should be considered with great caution where supply is greater than demand. If you reduce your price in order to stimulate extra demand, a competitor will suffer a volume decline. The only way that the competitor can regain the lost volume is by matching or beating your price reductions. This can quickly turn into a price war in which the only winners are the customers. They just sit on the fence and watch the suppliers strangle each other.

You might need an Accountant (Temporarily)

The title and intent of this book are dedicated to saving you the cost of internal and expensive financial skills. Nevertheless, you need to X-ray the products and services that you offer. To cost products or services accurately in a complex organisation takes a lot of time and some computer skills. There is a danger that, if you devote a lot of time to assembling reliable product costs, then other, equally important, tasks will be neglected. It is wise to consider the possibility of engaging temporary help to prepare the costings. The number of business failures and rationalisations is such that there are many competent accountants looking for project work who would be happy to develop your costing system at a reasonable price. The cost should not exceed £2,000. It would be money well spent if the alternative was to neglect customer service while you prepare the costing system yourself.

SUMMARY

Most businesses sell more than one product or service. It is not always obvious which products or customers are the most profitable. In the past, wholesalers and retailers tended to allocate overhead to products in proportion to the materials they bought. Equally, manufacturers tended to allocate overhead in proportion to direct labour. In the current competitive world, these approaches lead to incorrect product costs. Most businesses now spend a greater proportion of their money on overheads and a lesser proportion on direct labour. The key reason for this is automation. The old-fashioned approaches will not provide a reliable basis on which to make outsourcing and promotional decisions. An activity based, cost centre approach is needed to help you address these issues. The sequence for attributing the activity costs to products is:

(a) material costs;

(b) people costs;

(c) facilities costs;

(d) technology costs.

ABC is here to stay. Without it you will be at a serious competitive disadvantage. You only need to answer one question. What is the most effective way to introduce this cost system to your business? Then go and introduce it.

CHAPTER 9

MAKE THE RIGHT CAPITAL INVESTMENTS: THE TRANSPLANT

To stay competitive any business must be prepared to invest in new technology, for which funds are needed. They are sourced from retained earnings, capital grants, and long-term loans. The owners must ensure that the case for each proposed capital investment is sound. This is not just because the providers of funds will demand a convincing case, it is even more important that the owners will obtain an adequate reward in the form of additional revenue, lower costs or a combination of both.

Sometimes a person needs a transplant. It becomes necessary when an organ fails. Fixed assets are the organs of a business. They too may need to be expanded or replaced. There are four main types of asset transplants.

1. Purchase of new equipment to replace what is worn out.

2. Introduction of new technology to enhance your competitive position.

3. Purchases of assets required to create new products or services.

4. Statutory investments, such as pollution control.

The first three types of investment only make sense when they add to the profitability of a business, by either adding revenue or subtracting cost.

Jean Bigger owns a small and profitable manufacturing company. She recently visited a trade fair and saw two machines that would enhance profitability. When she returned to work she suggested the two investments to her factory manager. He was excited at the prospect of a transplant of new and effective technology. The investments cost £50,000 and £40,000 respectively. Jean's instincts told her that they were attractive. However, she could only afford to spend £50,000 on capital investment. She wondered which of the two investment proposals would be more beneficial to her business. She decided to prepare an appraisal of the costs and savings to validate her instincts. In consultation with the production manager, she prepared the forecasts in Table 9.1 and 9.2.

Table 9.1: Example of Jean Bigger's Investment Forecasts – Machine A

Year	1	2	3	4	5	Total
Operative wages [1]	14,500	14,863	15,234	15,615	16,005	76,217
Maintenance contract	2,500	2,500	2,500	2,500	2,500	12,500
Power [1]	1,500	1,538	1,576	1,615	1,656	7,885
Space [1]	1,000	1,025	1,051	1,077	1,104	5,257
Depreciation	10,000	10,000	10,000	10,000	10,000	50,000
Interest	5,000	4,000	3,000	2,000	1,000	15,000
Total	34,500	33,926	33,361	32,807	32,265	166,859
Less saving	31,000	33,825	36,772	39,845	43,049	184,491
Net profit (loss)	-3,500	-101	3,411	7,038	10,784	17,632

[1] Costs adjusted by 2.5% per annum to reflect forecast inflation.

Table 9.2: Example of Jean Bigger's Investment Forecasts – Machine B

Year	1	2	3	4	Total
Operative wages [1]	12,000	12,300	12,608	12,923	49,831
Maintenance contract	2,000	2,000	2,000	2,000	8,000
Power [1]	1,200	1,230	1,261	1,292	4,983
Space [1]	800	820	841	862	3,323
Depreciation	10,000	10,000	10,000	10,000	40,000
Interest	4,000	3,000	2,000	1,000	10,000
Total	30,000	29,350	28,710	28,077	116,137
Less saving [1]	31,000	31,775	32,569	33,384	128,728
Net profit	1,000	2,425	3,859	5,307	12,591

[1] Costs adjusted by 2.5% per annum to reflect forecast inflation.

Jean was delighted to find that the forecasts confirmed her instinctive diagnosis. She noted that machine A promised a higher profit than machine B. Before taking a final decision Jean felt that, with so much money at stake, she should have the proposals examined by a financial expert. She submitted the cost and saving forecasts to Vetters Consultants. Some days later she received the following report.

Report from Vetters Consultants

Vetters Consultants
Dublin 2

Ms J Bigger
Growing Close
Bradford

Dear Ms Bigger,
I have examined your proposed investment and report as follows.

1. I have calculated the financial returns using three appraisal tools. The calculations are shown in detail in an appendix. The results are as follows.

	Machine A	**Machine B**
Payback	3.43 years	2.60 years
Net present value	£10,802	£9,439
Profitability index	21.6	23.6

When assessing capital investment proposals the most important issues to consider are: how quickly you will get your money back and which proposal is intrinsically more profitable. Payback answers the first question. It favours machine B. Profitability index answers the second proposal. It also favours machine B. Since you told me that only £50,000 was available for capital investment, I recommend that you arrange to purchase machine B.

2. If you are satisfied that the cost and saving projections you prepared are correct, and could arrange £90,000 for capital investment you might also decide to buy machine A. However, I feel it is wise to point out two important risk factors that are relevant to the £90,000 expenditure. Firstly, the payback on machine A is arguably too long for a technology that is advancing rapidly. If a better machine comes on the market within the next two years you will regret the fact that you invested. Secondly, the purchase of both machines will place substantial pressure on your financial stability. Gearing will increase. Interest cover will

decline as the initial loss predicted for machine A combines with an additional interest charge of £9,000. If you wanted to buy both machines you should present the proposals to your bank and support them with budgeted financial statements:

(a) profit and loss accounts;
(b) balance sheets;
(c) cash flow forecasts.

If the bank support the proposals you might undertake the two investments.

3. If you invest it will mean that you cannot expect to have funds for other opportunities for at least eighteen months. You need to be confident that no essential capital investments will emerge during this period.

4. I note that you have not made a contingency allowance in preparing your forecasts. When you acquire a new technology you sometimes incur unforeseen expenditure. Simple examples include things, such as air-conditioning, reinforced flooring and pollution control. It might be a good idea to contact other businesses that have installed similar equipment in order to avoid expensive surprises.

If you have any queries please let me know.

Yours sincerely
A Vetter
Managing Partner

Appendix to Vetter's Report

The first step is to calculate the operating cash flow for each proposal. To do this I added back depreciation and interest. This was necessary because the best evaluation tools are based on operating cash flow (see Tables 9.3 and 9.4).

Table 9.3: Vetter's Investment Forecast – Machine A

Year	1	2	3	4	5	Total
Profit before tax	(3,500)	(101)	3,411	7,038	10,784	17,632
Interest	5,000	4,000	3,000	2,000	1,000	15,000
Depreciation	10,000	10,000	10,000	10,000	10,000	50,000
Operating cash flow	11,500	13,899	16,411	19,038	21,784	82,632

Table 9.4: Vetters' Investment Forecast – Machine B

Year	1	2	3	4	Total
Profit before tax	1,000	2,425	3,859	5,307	12,591
Interest	4,000	3,000	2,000	1,000	10,000
Depreciation	10,000	10,000	10,000	10,000	40,000
Operating cash flow	15,000	15,425	15,859	16,307	62,591

1. Payback

Payback compares the operating cash flow with the investment cost.

The quicker you get your money back the lower the risk

	Machine A	Machine B
Investment	50,000	40,000
Cash year one	11,500	15,000
Exposure	38,500	25,000
Cash year two	13,899	15,425
Exposure	24,601	9,575
Cash year three	16,411	15,859
Exposure	8,190	
Cash year four	19,038	

Payback period $\quad 3 + \dfrac{8,190}{19,038} = 3.43$ years $\qquad 2 + \dfrac{9,575}{15,859} = 2.6$ years

Payback favours machine B. It takes 2.6 years to recover your money. While payback suggests that machine B is safer, it does not tell you

it is better. I regard a payback period in excess of three years, from
an investment in rapidly changing technology, as too long. However, you need to look at the other appraisal tools before making a
final decision.

Running is often recommended as an excellent way to fitness
and health. In running terms, payback is equivalent to a 100 metre
sprint. The record time is judged by the speed at which the cash
inflows will repay the capital invested. Payback ignores cash flows
beyond the time when the cost of the investment is recovered. This
limitation is best managed by using net present value (NPV) as well
as payback.

2. Net Present Value

Net present value is the best measure of a capital investment. It
compares the cash you spend with the cash you will recover as you
use the asset. However, since it will take time to get the cash back a
correction factor has to be applied. This converts the future cash
inflows into their value today. It is like saying that if I give you
£50,000 then you will give me £60,802. The calculations are in Tables
9.5 and 9.6.

Table 9.5: Vetters' Assessment of Net Present Value – Machine A

Year	Cash return	Discount factor [1]	Present Value
1	11,500	0.9091	10,455
2	13,899	0.8265	11,488
3	16,411	0.7513	12,330
4	19,038	0.6830	13,003
5	21,784	0.6209	13,526
Present value of future net savings			60,802
Less invested			50,000
Net present value			10,802

[1] The reason for using this particular discount factor is explained later in this
chapter.

Table 9.6: Vetters' Assessment of Net Present Value – Machine A

Year	Cash return	Discount factor [1]	Present Value
1	15,000	0.9091	13,637
2	15,425	0.8265	12,749
3	15,859	0.7513	11,915
4	16,307	0.6830	11,138
Present value of future net savings			49,439
Less invested			40,000
Net present value			9,439

Net present value is equivalent to running a marathon. It looks at an investment over its operating life. Five years for machine A. Four years for machine B.

3. Profitability Index

At first glance it might appear that the higher net present value makes machine A the better investment opportunity. This conclusion is faulty. It fails to recognise that you will have to invest an extra £10,000 in order to earn the additional £1,363 of present value. My third tool, the profitability index, levels the playing pitch. It should be used in conjunction with net present value in all cases where the value of investment proposals exceeds the funds available to pay for them.

	Machine A	Machine B
Net present value	10,802	9,439
Divided by investment cost	50,000	40,000
Profitability index	21.6	23.6

When you are trying to decide which of several projects that are competing for funds is best, the simple rule is to select the one with the highest profitability index. The higher the profitability index, the greater the return per pound invested. Machine B, with a profitability index of £0.236, is better than machine A.

Jean discussed Vetters' report with her production manager. They felt that the payback information made sense. However, neither of them felt comfortable with net present value. They were not sure whether it should be interpreted as strongly encouraging the purchase of both machines or not. Jean decided to arrange a meeting with Vetters in order to clarify the position.

COMPUTING AND INTERPRETING NET PRESENT VALUE

As Vetters explained, net present value is designed to compare a current cash outflow with future cash inflows. In order to make the comparison sensible, the future inflows are discounted to their present value. The longer you have to wait to receive the cash returns, the greater will be the discount factor. To realise how NPV works we need to understand discounting. A reminder of the principles of compounding is the first step.

Compounding

Consider a simple question. What will you receive in one year's time if you deposit £1,000 at 10 per cent. The answer, £1,100 is simple arithmetic. Suppose you left the capital and interest on deposit for a further year you will receive £1,210. This is because you will earn 10 per cent on £1,100 in the second year. The calculation uses compounding. What will you receive in ten year's time if you leave the capital and interest on deposit? You need a calculator to get the answer £2,593.74. It is verified as follows.

Year 1	Deposit	1,000.00		Year 6	Deposit	1,610.51
	Interest	100.00			Interest	161.05
Year 2	Deposit	1,100.00		Year 7	Deposit	1,771.56
	Interest	110.00			Interest	177.16
Year 3	Deposit	1,210.00		Year 8	Deposit	1,948.72
	Interest	121.00			Interest	194.87
Year 4	Deposit	1,331.00		Year 9	Deposit	2,143.59
	Interest	133.10			Interest	214.36
Year 5	Deposit	1,464.10		Year 10	Deposit	2,357.95
	Interest	146.41			Interest	235.79
		1,610.51				2,593.74

The calculations can be simplified by using a formula from your schooldays.

$$A = P \times \left(1 + \frac{R}{100}\right)^n$$

In the above equation, A = future *Amount*, P = *Principal*, R = the *Rate* of interest and N = the *Number* of years. Solving the ten-year deposit, we find A = £1,000 x 1.1^{10} or £1,000 x 2.59374 = £2,593.74.

Discounting

Discounting is the reverse of compounding. If I told you that you would receive a guaranteed payment of £1,100 in one year's time, what is the maximum that you be prepared to offer for it now? If you require a return of ten per cent on any money you invest, the answer is £1,000. This reverses compounding. It is based on the formula.

$$P = \frac{A}{\left(1 + \frac{R}{100}\right)^n}$$

You Don't Need An Accountant

Using this formula we can convert future cash into its present value. If you require a return of 10 per cent you simply divide the cash promised by 1.1 for each year into the future. Since the calculations can become cumbersome, we will create a table of present values of £1 so as to simplify them (see Table 9.7).

Table 9.7: Present values of £1

Year	Discount Factor	Calculation	Year	Discount Factor	Calculation
1	0.909	(1 divided by 1.1)	6	0.564	(0.621 / 1.1)
2	0.826	(0.909 / 1.1)	7	0.513	(0.564 / 1.1)
3	0.751	(0.826 / 1.1)	8	0.467	(0.513 / 1.1)
4	0.683	(0.751 / 1.1)	9	0.424	(0.467 / 1.1)
5	0.621	(0.683 / 1.1)	10	0.386	(0.424 / 1.1)

In the appendix to Vetters' report, he used the first five factors in this table. The net present value that he calculated was based on the argument that to receive £11,500 in one year's time is equivalent to receiving £10,455 now. Vetters used a discount rate of 10 per cent to convert the future cash flows to present value. In current economic conditions this is correct. The rate is based on two factors: the interest on the money that you will borrow to fund the capital expenditure and the premium you require to justify investing in risky new technology rather than safer alternatives, such as government securities. If interest rates were to rise, the discount factor would have to be increased by a similar amount. Tables showing the discount factors at rates of up to 20 per cent are provided at the end of this chapter. Once you have correctly forecast the flows of cash that will arise, the NPV calculation is not difficult. Jean Bigger did the hard part by predicting the profits that will arise as a result of the machine purchases. If Jean made a mistake in her forecasts, it could mean that she will regret investing. If this happened, it would not be right to blame the capital investment tools or Vetters' use of them. The computer mnemonic garbage in, garbage out (GIGO) is very appropriate to investment appraisal.

Errors to avoid in Forecasting the Cash Flows

1. Where a capital investment will result in additional products for sale, it is vital to remember that you will have to invest in working capital as well as fixed assets. I have often seen the event that the business will have to pay suppliers and staff long before collections start flowing from

customers overlooked. In Chapter 3 we saw the damaging impact of growth on the cash resources of a business. To overlook the working capital element of an investment is an easy route to an overtrading crisis.

2. In his report, Vetters pointed out the importance of allowing for the unexpected. New initiatives often suffer from teething problems. Such problems usually result in extra costs or delayed benefits. A prudent analyst includes a contingency allowance.

3. Construction investments are notoriously difficult to plan and control. Delays in construction and changes in specification add to the cost.

Funding your Capital Investments Correctly

Healthy businesses often fail as a result of capital investments that are incorrectly funded. There are four attractive and two dangerous sources of funds.

Attractive
- Surplus cash.
- Term loans.
- Share issue proceeds.
- Capital grants.

Dangerous
- Bank overdrafts.
- Lengthened supplier credit.

The problem with the dangerous sources is that they can be recalled at short notice. Such funds are inappropriate for investments that will be slow to create cash. A good banker will be prepared to match the repayment schedule with your cash inflows. For example, Jean would not like to have to repay £10,000 of the loan in the first year. This would leave too little in reserve to cover unexpected costs. Delaying repayment will result in a higher interest bill. Nevertheless, it is wiser to accept this than to commit to an excessive repayment.

Jean felt that Vetters had made an excellent point when he advised her to include a contingency allowance. She felt that she should reconsider her repayment plan. She revised her repayment in Table 9.8.

You Don't Need An Accountant

Table 9.8 Jean Bigger's Revised Repayments

Machine B

Year	1	2	3	4	Total
Operative wages	12,000	12,300	12,608	12,923	49,831
Maintenance contract	2,000	2,000	2,000	2,000	8,000
Power	1,200	1,230	1,261	1,292	4,983
Space	800	820	841	862	3,323
Interest [1]	4,000	3,100	2,100	1,000	10,200
Total	20,000	19,450	18,810	18,077	76,337
Saving current technology	31,000	31,775	32,569	33,384	128,728
Surplus pre-loan repayment	11,000	12,325	13,759	15,307	52,391
Loan repayment	9,000	10,000	11,000	10,000	40,000
Contingency fund	2,000	2,325	2,759	5,307	12,391

[1] Interest was calculated at 10% on the balance outstanding.

If no unexpected cash costs occur the surplus cash in the contingency fund will earn some interest. This will off-set part of the extra interest, which she will have to pay.

TWO ADDITIONAL INVESTMENT APPRAISAL TOOLS

Vetters' report did not discuss two other tools frequently used by financial controllers. The first is internal rate of return (IRR). This is the maximum rate of interest that a project can afford to pay and repay the loan in full. IRR is easy to calculate using a computer spreadsheet. For example, Vetters could compute the IRR for machine A using Microsoft Excel as follows.

Cell	Input
C1	-50000
C2	11500
C3	13899
C4	16411
C5	19038
C6	21784
C7	=IRR(c1:c6)

When enter is pressed, after placing the formula in cell C7, the IRR 17 per cent will be reported. If you want the IRR to be more accurate, you simply format cell C7 to several decimal places. Table 9.9 shows the exact IRR, 17.2526 per cent. The cash inflows are used to repay interest and capital.

Table 9.9: Internal Rate of Return

Borrow		50,000	End year three loan		32,081
Surplus cash	11,500		Surplus cash	19.038	
Interest at 17.2526%	8,626		Interest at 17.2526%	5,535	
Loan repaid		2,874	Loan repaid		13,503
End year one loan		47,126	End year four loan		18.578
Surplus cash	13,899		Surplus cash	21,784	
Interest at 17.2526%	8,130		Interest at 17.2526%	3,206	
Loan repaid		5,769	Loan repaid		18,578
End year two loan		41,357	End year five loan		0
Surplus cash	16,411				
Interest at 17.2526%	7,135				
Loan repaid		9,276			
End year three loan		32,081			

Some commentators have criticised IRR on the grounds that it expects the cash inflows to earn interest at the IRR rate. Table 9.10 illustrates this defect. It separates the cash flows into a deposit and a borrowing pool. It then charges and credits interest at the IRR. The model assumes that no loan repayments are made through the life of the project and that the deposit pool of £110,810 is used to clear the loan.

9.10: Separated Cash Flow with Interest at IRR

Deposit Pool		Borrowing Pool	
Cash flow year one	11,500	Borrow	50,000
Interest 17.25%	1,984	Interest 17.25%	8,626
Cash flow year two	13,899	Total loan	58,626
Total deposit	27,383	Interest 17.25%	10,115
Interest 17.25%	4,724	Total loan	68,741
Cash flow year three	16,411	Interest 17.25%	11,859
Total deposit	48,518	Total loan	80,600
Interest 17.25%	8,371	Interest 17.25%	13,906
Cash flow year four	19,038	Total loan	94,506
Total deposit	75,927	Interest 17.25%	16,304
Interest 17.25%	13,099	Loan repaid	110,810
Cash flow year five	21,784		
Total deposit	110,810		

The IRR tells Jean she could afford to borrow £50,000 at 17.25 per cent and just be able to repay it in full. The IRR for machine B is 20.33 per cent.

Modified internal rate of return (MIRR) has recently been developed to overcome the defect in internal rate of return. MIRR establishes the maximum rate of interest you can afford to pay assuming that the deposit pool earns interest at the company profit rate, in this case 10 per cent. Using Microsoft Excel, Vetters calculated the MIRR. It was 14.39 per cent for machine A and 15.98 per cent for machine B. He used the following inputs to his Excel spreadsheet:

Cell	Input
C1	-50000
C2	11500
C3	13899
C4	16411
C5	19038
C6	21784
C7	= MIRR(c1:c6, ·1, ·1)

When you press enter, after placing the formula in cell C7 and set the display to two decimal places, the MIRR is shown at 14.39 per cent. This level of accuracy is needed to illustrate the MIRR in Table 9.11.

9.11: Excel Spreadsheat for MIRR

Deposit Pool		Borrowing Pool	
Cash flow year one	11,500	Borrow	50,000
Add interest at 10%	1,150	Interest at 14.39%	7,194
Cash flow year two	13,899	Total loan	57,194
Total on deposit	26,549	Interest at 14.39%	8,229
Add interest 10%	2,655	Total loan	65,423
Cash flow year three	16,411	Interest at 14.39%	9,413
Total on deposit	45,615	Total loan	74,836
Add interest 10%	4,562	Interest at 14.39%	10,767
Cash flow year four	19,038	Total loan	85,603
Total on deposit	69,215	Interest at 14.39%	12,317
Add interest 10%	6,921	Loan repaid	97,920
Cash flow year five	21,784		
Total deposit	97,920		

Contrast this with the 17.25 per cent that the deposits are assumed to earn in the IRR. You can practice IRR and MIRR by putting the data for machine B into a spreadsheet. Your answers should be IRR 20.33 per cent and MIRR 15.98 per cent.

How to plan and Evaluate Capital Investment Correctly

The planning and control of capital investment is a three-stage process.

1. *The first step is to predict the amount of money that will be available for capital investment.* This is a combination of the untied retained earnings, the amount of term borrowing that can be piggybacked on this without letting gearing become excessive and the amount of capital grants that can be arranged to support the fixed asset purchases.

2. *The second step is to set appropriate accept and reject criterion.* Start by setting your payback criterion. In an industry that is evolving rapidly, such as computer software, the payback would be set at two years. At the other end of the scale a new runway at an airport could not reasonably be expected to repay the capital investment in less than fifteen years and the landing fees can be confidently predicted. You must decide the appropriate time scale and stick to it. Any project that fails to meet your payback target should be discarded. You need not go to the trouble of preparing more complex evaluations. If the payback is acceptable, then the net present value method should also be calculated. A discount factor of 10 per cent is suitable with interest rates at their present level. Any project in which the present value of the future cash inflows exceeds the cost of the investment will be profitable. Remember to use the profitability index if the supply of investments exceeds the funds that will be available. The higher the index, the better the project. If you are used to working with spreadsheets, you should also compute the MIRR. The higher the interest rate you can afford, the better the project.

3. *Remember that any appraisal tool is only as good as the cash forecasts that will be used in it.* For example, if Jean Bigger underestimated the costs or overestimated the operating life she might wind up backing a project that should not have been supported. Remember the GIGO mnemonic, 'garbage in garbage out'.

SUMMARY

Capital investment is the transplant of new fixed assets onto a business. We are all sadly aware of instances of the failure of organ transplants. Business transplants are also risky. For example, a decision to make a large capital investment that turns sour is one of the easiest ways to wreck a healthy business. You need to shine up your crystal ball to predict the cash flows accurately. You need not include depreciation in your basic cash flows. The cash is spent when you pay for the asset. The evaluation compares cash in against cash out. Equally, you should not include interest in your basic cash flows. The discount factor that you apply to the future cash inflows corrects for the interest cost. The most important tools of project appraisal are:

- payback;

- net present value.

If these tools say you should reject a project, then you should walk away. Liquidators are kept busy winding up businesses that should have rejected major capital investment proposals. If you have spreadsheet skills you should also compute the MIRR (see Table 9.11).

Table 9.12: Discount Factors at Rates from 8 per cent to 20 per cent

Year	8%	9%	10%	11%	12%	13%	14%	15%	16%	17%	18%	19%	20%
1	0.926	0.917	0.909	0.901	0.893	0.885	0.877	0.870	0.862	0.855	0.847	0.840	0.833
2	0.857	0.842	0.826	0.812	0.797	0.783	0.769	0.756	0.743	0.731	0.718	0.706	0.694
3	0.794	0.772	0.751	0.731	0.712	0.693	0.675	0.658	0.641	0.624	0.609	0.593	0.579
4	0.735	0.708	0.683	0.659	0.636	0.613	0.592	0.572	0.552	0.534	0.516	0.499	0.482
5	0.681	0.650	0.621	0.593	0.567	0.543	0.519	0.497	0.476	0.456	0.437	0.419	0.402
6	0.630	0.596	0.564	0.535	0.507	0.480	0.456	0.432	0.410	0.390	0.370	0.352	0.335
7	0.583	0.547	0.513	0.482	0.452	0.425	0.400	0.376	0.354	0.333	0.314	0.296	0.279
8	0.540	0.502	0.467	0.434	0.404	0.376	0.351	0.327	0.305	0.285	0.266	0.249	0.233
9	0.500	0.460	0.424	0.391	0.361	0.333	0.308	0.284	0.263	0.243	0.225	0.209	0.194
10	0.463	0.422	0.386	0.352	0.322	0.295	0.270	0.247	0.227	0.208	0.191	0.176	0.162
11	0.429	0.388	0.350	0.317	0.287	0.261	0.237	0.215	0.195	0.178	0.162	0.148	0.135
12	0.397	0.356	0.319	0.286	0.257	0.231	0.208	0.187	0.168	0.152	0.137	0.124	0.112
13	0.368	0.326	0.290	0.258	0.229	0.204	0.182	0.163	0.145	0.130	0.116	0.104	0.093
14	0.340	0.299	0.263	0.232	0.205	0.181	0.160	0.141	0.125	0.111	0.099	0.088	0.078
15	0.315	0.275	0.239	0.209	0.183	0.160	0.140	0.123	0.108	0.095	0.084	0.074	0.065
16	0.292	0.252	0.218	0.188	0.163	0.141	0.123	0.107	0.093	0.081	0.071	0.062	0.054
17	0.270	0.231	0.198	0.170	0.146	0.125	0.108	0.093	0.080	0.069	0.060	0.052	0.045
18	0.250	0.212	0.180	0.153	0.130	0.111	0.095	0.081	0.069	0.059	0.051	0.044	0.038
19	0.232	0.194	0.164	0.138	0.116	0.098	0.083	0.070	0.060	0.051	0.043	0.037	0.031
20	0.215	0.178	0.149	0.124	0.104	0.087	0.073	0.061	0.051	0.043	0.037	0.031	0.026

CHAPTER 10

SPENDING CAN DAMAGE YOUR HEALTH: DIETARY PRECAUTIONS

Everybody knows that excessive weight can place pressure on the heart. If the weight is not tackled by appropriate dietary measures the consequences can be fatal. In the same way, a financial doctor is concerned about cost fat. This fat makes a business flabby and uncompetitive. Most businesses have substantial cost fat. It must be tackled professionally if the organisation is to become leaner and fitter.

Jack High distributes bowls equipment. He recently had a benchmarking exercise carried out on his business. The following is the consultant's report.

Vetters Consultants
Dublin 2

Mr J High
Green Road
London

Dear Mr High,

I benchmarked your business in line with your instructions. It was not possible to get sufficient detail of the make-up of your competitor's cost to enable me to pinpoint exactly where the excesses exist. Nevertheless, you are achieving a pre-tax profit of only 2.7 per cent and this is 7.2 per cent below the industry average. Table 10.1 summarises the data.

Table 10.1: Jack High's Profits compared with the Industry Average

	Jack High		The Industry [1]	
	£	% sales	£ %	sales
Sales	371,058	100.0	3,306,105	100.0
Cost of sales	256,029	69.0	2,347,475	71.0
Gross margin	115,029	31.0	958,630	29.0
Overheads	105,010	28.3	631,326	19.1
Net margin	10,019	2.7	327,304	9.9

[1] Data excludes many small dealers that operate from home.

Your gross margin at 31 per cent compares favourably with competitors. It is your support overhead at 28.3 per cent of sales compared with 19.1 per cent for the industry that is damaging profitability. These costs need to be systematically attacked.

The most widespread sources of excess cost are:
- overtime payments;
- interest costs;
- energy costs.

These are the areas that should be addressed in the first instance. You will need a very creative process if you are to locate ways of saving expenditure in these and other areas. The key question that you must constantly pose is whether spending can be reduced without causing damage to quality or customer service. If you like, I can arrange for one of my staff to help you to identify specific and effective cost saving initiatives. However, this would involve you in substantial expense at a time when cost containment is your top priority. In the circumstances it is probably wiser for you to mastermind the process yourself.

If I can be of further help in this matter please contact me.

Yours sincerely,
A Vetters
Managing Partner

Jack is not alone in needing a new cost diet. Even the most professional organisations spend at least 2 per cent on things that provide poor value. This may sound surprising but there are a number of plausible, albeit unacceptable, explanations.

Sentiments that can point to Poor Value for Money

1. 'That's how we always did it.' Hardly a good reason for missing a better way.

2. 'The customers/staff won't like it.' This reinforces an inefficient status quo!

3. 'It will never work.' Another way to preserve an inefficient status quo.

4. 'We spent good money on this. We must continue to use it even if the decision to invest has proved unwise.'

5. 'I added 2.5 per cent to last year's cost. This will cover inflation.' Not all costs follow the general rate of inflation.

6. 'I like to have a fair amount of stock on hand. You never know when we might get a large order if we could deliver immediately.' Even when so many companies are finding that JIT really works!

7. Many attractive cost reduction ideas, such as buying fixed assets and paying redundancy packages, require an up-front investment in order to provide ongoing savings. If a business cannot afford the up front investment, the idea may wither away on the back burner.

The Keys to Value for Money

1. To increase cost is not a sin provided you increase revenue by more.

2. To reduce revenue is not a sin provided you decrease cost by more.

3. Co-operation with suppliers and customers can lead to significant savings which can be shared by participants in the value chain.

4. Excessive cost is caused by strategy, capacity and people. It is only by quantifying it using activity based costing, that we can start to tackle it constructively.

5. Most people in a company have good ideas of how to improve value for money. They do not always share them. Carefully managed consultation is required if the good ideas are to be surfaced and actioned.

How to identify Cost Waste

There are four steps in the battle to get value for money from your spending.

Step 1: Predict the cost. In Chapter 8 we saw that most businesses plan and record spending by expenditure type rather than activity type. This is not likely to help you to pinpoint all waste. Activity based costing is an important plank in the quest for value for money.

Step 2: The second part of the search for value is to list the activity based costs in order of significance starting with the biggest and ending with the smallest. Table 10.2 provides a summarised example.

Table 10.2: Activity Based Costs in Descending Order

	Activity	Per Cent of Total	Excl. Top Two
Direct material	372,156	54.0	
Direct labour basic pay	80,345	11.7	
Marketing	67,105	9.7	28.4
Power	33,814	4.9	14.3
Overtime	25,369	3.7	10.7
Quality control	19,162	2.8	8.1
Shift premiums	18,025	2.6	7.6
Delivery	14,358	2.1	6.1
Product design	11,128	1.6	4.7
Fringe pay costs	10,635	1.5	4.5
Bookkeeping	9,610	1.4	4.1
Material handling	7,204	1.0	3.0
Sundries	19,877	3.0	8.5
	688,788	100.0	100.0

The column headed 'excluding the top two' is prepared because in most organisations the top two tend to involve the lion's share of spending and blur the significance of other costs. The overall table seems to suggest that power is a relatively unimportant cost amounting to 4.9 per cent of budgeted spending. In the excluding top two column, it amounts to 14.3 per cent of spending and is, therefore, pinpointed as highly significant.

Step 3: The third step in the search for value for money is highly judgmental. It should involve all of your staff. Ask each staff member to pinpoint three cost areas that they feel provide poor value for money. Of course, some will suggest things such as the owner's car. Such comments may be ill-judged. However, even these provide insights into different people's perspective of the business. It is astonishing how often this type of research highlights good cost saving ideas. Furthermore, if a staff member makes a worthwhile cost saving suggestion, I firmly believe that they should be rewarded with a share of the expense saved.

Step 4: The final step in the search for value for money is to slot all the data into a cost reduction matrix (see Figure 10.1). I developed this idea from the standard four box model used in areas such as the Boston Consulting Group product portfolio. To enter a cost in the matrix you must first decide whether it is significant or not. All costs that represent more than 2 per cent of total spending, excluding the top two, are significant. They will be placed in one or other of the top quadrants. Secondly, based on your cost waste survey, you must classify costs that provide good and poor value for money. Costs that provide poor value for money are placed in the left hand quadrants. The rules for completing the matrix are:

• more than 2 per cent of spending and good value for money (top right).

• more than 2 per cent of spending and poor value for money (top left).

• less than 2 per cent of spending and good value for money (bottom right).

• less than 2 per cent of spending and poor value for money (bottom left).

Figure 10.1: Cost Reduction Matrix

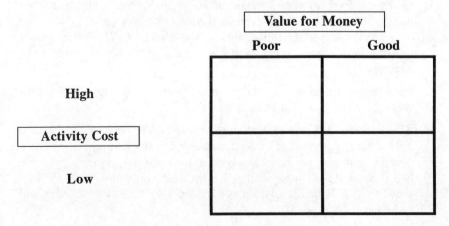

Expenditure in the top left quadrant should be a key target. Spending is significant and offers poor value for money. These are the premier league costs. Once one is pinpointed all the organisation's energy should be devoted to re-engineering it to provide better value.

Six Reasons for Excessive Cost

1. **Poor timing of asset replacement decisions.** To replace fixed assets too early adds substantial cost but does not confer adequate technological/competitive benefit. Replacing assets too late leads to uncompetitive costs. High quality investment appraisal, dealt with in Chapter 9, is the key to timing replacement decisions correctly.

2. **Over luxurious assets.** It is astonishing how many businesses that fail have assets that are too luxurious. 'Rolls Royce' standard, head offices, company cars, corporate hospitality, and other trappings of wealth are often used to send signals of prosperity that may not be justified by the facts.

3. **Under-utilised capacity.** People, plant and space cost money even when they are not being used. You can't afford sleeping capacity. The first step in the battle to use it profitably is to know its cost. This often proves difficult to calculate. The cost of idle capacity is dealt with later in the chapter.

4. **Poor product design.** A good product design will help to avoid expensive off-cuts and similar sources of waste.

5. **Absence of a JIT ethos.** Holding stock is very expensive. The annual holding cost is in excess of 20 per cent of the stock value. During this decade, immense savings have been made by many organisations that had previously maintained that just-in-time could not work in their industry. All it needs is a proper partnership between supplier and customer.

6. **Inadequate controls.** Every organisation must find the delicate balance between the cost of prevention and the penalty for failure. For example, auditors worry about internal control. To have separate people bill customers and manage cash is a sound principle but a luxury that most small businesses cannot afford.

The Value Chain Perspective

A significant cause of excess cost is failure to look at spending in the value chain. You look for cost savings that can result from an effective partnership with suppliers or customers. Hergert and Morris[1] provide a superb example. It reduced costs and increased profits in both supplier and customer. Chocolate was supplied to a confectionery manufacturer in solid blocks, value chain analysis showed that delivery in liquid form would save bulking and packing for the supplier and unwrapping and melting for the customer.

Figure 10.2: Duplicated Costs in the Confectionary Industry

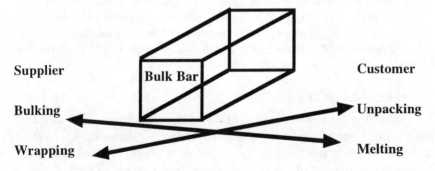

Supplier	Bulk Bar	Customer
Bulking		Unpacking
Wrapping		Melting

The value chain points you toward ways to avoid duplicated effort. It should also help you to reduce expensive waste. For example, a computer aided design package can help to avoid off-cuts in the textile and furniture industries.

Process Analysis

One way to structure your thinking, so as to find creative ideas that yield improved value for money, is the process analysis model (see Figure 10.3).

---

1. 'Accounting for Value Chain Analysis' *Strategic Management Journal* (1989) Vol. 10.

Figure 10.3: Process Analysis Model

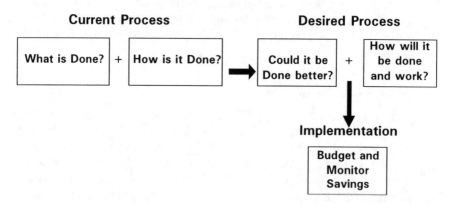

The desired process is the challenging part of this analysis. It requires great creativity to identify ways of doing things better. An interesting example is that of a client of mine who took delivery of large volumes of oil for use in manufacturing. An imaginative engineer recognised that the actual volume received was influenced by the air temperature at the time of delivery. It only required a small step to work out a conversion factor to adjust the volume for air temperature. This idea resulted in a worthwhile increase in the volume received at the relevant price per litre.

Managing Idle Capacity

It is difficult to get a perfect match between capacity and customer demand. Most organisations give too little attention to the fact that assets are costing money even when they are not in use. Standard costing and activity based costing help to quantify the cost of idle capacity. Awareness of the magnitude of the cost is the first step to avoiding somnolent assets. Many organisations are in a position in which ability to supply exceeds customer demand. They try to recover their cost penalties in selling prices. Customers rebel. They won't pay for idle capacity as 'tuned-in' competitors offer keener prices. The first step is to quantify the idle capacity. If a large cost penalty exists, then the second step must be to find ways to use it profitably or to eliminate it. Consider a machine with a capacity to run for 8,640 hours in a year (360 working days of 24 hours each) and a budgeted usage of 5,000 hours. The costs are:

Operator	56,160
Power	16,800
Maintenance	7,200
Space	17,280
Depreciation	43,200
	140,640

A 'normal' machine hour rate of £28.128 recovers the running costs if planned hours are achieved. This rate imposes an unfair penalty on products that 'buy' the machine hours. The machine is costing money even when idle: operatives are still being paid, space is driving costs such as rates and insurance, and obsolescence, which drives depreciation, is drawing closer. A more correct charge rate is computed as in Table 10.3.

Table 10.3: Cost of Idle Capacity

	Total £	Utilised £	Idle £
Operator	56,160	32,500	23,660
Power (5,000 hours)	16,800	16,800	—
Maintenance (5,000 hours)	7,200	7,200	—
Space	17,280	10,000	7,280
Depreciation	43,200	25,000	18,200
	140,640	91,500	49,140

Dividing the cost of utilised capacity by the planned running hours gives a correct machine hour rate of £18.30. Identifying the £49,140 cost of idle capacity is the first step to managing it properly.

Sourcing Policy

A notable feature of world class manufacturing is the switch to outsourcing. Decisions of this kind have traditionally been made using relevant costs (i.e. costs that would be avoided if the organisation switched from in-house to subcontract or vice versa). Relevant cost analysis usually fails to recognise the multiplicity of costs involved in making a component.

Relevant costs	Make	Buy
Material	5,126	11,500
Labour	3,986	
Energy	1,429	
Facilities	1,809	
	12,350	

Based on this data it is clearly cheaper to outsource.

The Issues in 'Make Versus Buy'

Make	Buy
Longer cycle time	Shorter cycle time
Low volumes required	Economies of scale
Increased number of procurements	Single procurements
Additional space	Management issues

Decisions to outsource should reflect these support cost implications. Unless your measurement is accurate your make and buy strategy may be incorrect. Activity based costing is a vital input into such decisions.

Advantages and Disadvantages of Outsourcing

+ Process simplification	– Risk of poor quality
+ Convert fixed to variable	– Ability to respond to crisis reduced
+ Reduce space requirements	– Problems in changeover
+ Pay as you use	– Creates idle capacity to be tackled
+ Allows greater concentration on core mission	

Support Costs that might be outsourced profitably

Often outsourced	Seldom considered
Catering	Bulk mailing
Cleaning	Credit control
Delivery	Design
Equipment maintenance	Human resources
Grounds maintenance	Internal audit
Security	Management accounting
	Payroll

Cost/benefit Mismatch

Quality management offers excellent examples of the delicate balance between cost and benefit. Juran[2] shows the two key elements.

Conformance	Failure
Prevention	Internal costs
Appraisal	External costs

---

2. 'The Quality Edge: A Management Tool' (PIMA, 1985).

Prevention and appraisal costs are the expenses related to conformance with quality standards. Failure costs arise through non-conformance. As voluntary spending on prevention and appraisal rises, the cost of non-conformance should decline more quickly. The optimum cost of quality occurs where the marginal cost of prevention exactly equals the marginal cost of failure.

The Components of the Cost of Quality

Prevention cost

Design review

Operative training

Preventive maintenance

Quality assurance

Appraisal cost

Sampling

Testing

Inspection

Internal failure cost

Scrap

Rework

Downtime

External failure cost

Warranties

Product recall

Loss of customer goodwill

Field service

It is vital to recognise that certain prevention costs are once-off. Since they result in ongoing savings by avoiding the risk of failure they are very attractive.

Figure 10.4: The Quality Balancing Trick

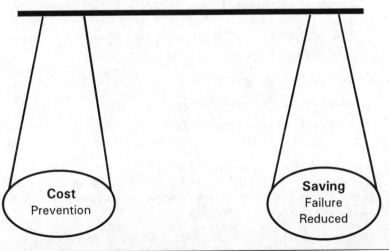

If prevention spending rises then cost of failures should fall.

There are numerous aspects of your business where cost benefit analyses can prove rewarding. Fertile areas include:

(a) all aspects of insurance;

(b) treasury management;

(c) internal audit.

Customer Care and Value for Money

Research in the USA pinpoints the importance of keeping your customers. There are four key rules.

1. **The rule of 25 : 25** You lose and gain 25 per cent of your customers each year.

2. **The rule of 20 : 25** If the rate of customer loss could be reduced to 20 per cent, then profits would increase by 25 per cent.

3. **The rule of 5 : 1** To recruit a new customer costs five times as much as to retain an existing one.

4. **The rule of 225 : 20** The top 20 per cent of customers yield 225 per cent of profits. Heavy losses are incurred by selling to the lowest quartile.

Twelve Practical Suggestions

1. Turn off light and heat when not required. It never fails to amaze me how many office blocks are lit up at night when clearly empty.

2. Monitor the cost and need for travel tightly. The Gulf War caused many companies to suspend non-urgent air travel. When the War ended many businesses looked at the reduction in expenses and started to question whether many of the flights were really necessary.

3. Divert communications from phone and post to fax and e-mail.

4. Untidiness wastes time and money.

5. Value your cars in the right insurance bands. The cost of a policy may fall dramatically if the insured value is reduced from £20,500 to £19,900.

6. Revisit lease and buy decisions regularly. Many companies have a rule such as 'we lease all cars' or 'we buy all cars'. The decision may have been correct when the policy was introduced. Passage of time may have eroded the competitive advantage.

7. Outlaw overtime. This requires careful planning and control.

8. Never permit budget extrapolation. Bids must include a review of alternative ways to achieve the end.

9. Devote 20 per cent of time at management meetings to tackling idle capacity.

10. Improve treasury management:
    - better cash forecasting;
    - investigating economic sources of funds;
    - active management of currency and interest rate exposures.

11. Review your needs for secondary facilities. They cause:
    - rent and rates;
    - light, heat, insurance, etc.;
    - security.

12. Start meetings on time. Calculate the total pay cost for each meeting. Publicise it.

SUMMARY

Everybody knows that excessive weight places undue pressure on the heart. Similarly, businesses tend to carry cost flab. A medical doctor and a financial doctor will prescribe a healthy diet. Most organisations get poor value for money from some of their spending. There are many reasons. Among them, the greatest is a failure to recognise that the same end can often be achieved more cheaply and effectively. Even large organisations lurch from one cost reduction programme to the next. This reflects a failure to recognise that new and simple ways are emerging that will make a business more efficient. A 'that's the way we always did it' attitude guarantees failure in the quest for value for money.

The cost reduction matrix helps to identify activities where the amount spent is high, while the value for money is poor. Even in large companies cost effective opportunities to outsource, automate and re-engineer are frequently missed. The cause is usually either lack of imagination or lack of information. Adding 2 per cent onto your net margin might be the difference between struggling and thriving. It should be available if you are prepared to search for it.

A special diet designed to identify and reduce cost 'fat' is an essential part of corporate health.

CHAPTER 11

ENHANCE SHAREHOLDER VALUE TAKE A LONG VIEW: GUIDE TO A HEALTHY FUTURE

If you invest in a successful business, you will be paid dividends. If you invest in a government stock, you will receive interest. Since a business investment is more risky, you might expect it to provide a higher cash return. It won't. The dividend yield is the best way to assess the cash return from an investment. It is calculated by dividing the latest dividend by the current share price. The dividend yield you will get from investing in 'blue chip' companies is currently about 2 per cent. This compares unfavourably with the interest rate, of about 7 per cent, you can get from investing in government stocks.

There is a simple explanation for this surprising gap. Government stock offers limited opportunities for capital appreciation. This is because, at the end of the period of issue, the stock is redeemed at par. As a result the bulk of the return an investor receives is the fixed interest paid. By contrast, when an investor buys shares in a successful business they hope for rising profits and increasing dividends. Furthermore, if they sell the shares, they hope to receive more than the purchase price. This capital appreciation must be taken into account when calculating the real return. Consider an example.

1. Shares purchased three years ago 1,000 at £2.40 each.

2. Dividends per share: year one 4.8p, year two 5.2p, year three 5.6p.

3. Shares sold today 1,000 at £3 each.

The return you received from the investment can be calculated as follows.

Dividends	year one	48.00
	year two	52.00
	year three	56.00
Capital gain		<u>600.00</u>
Total pre-tax return		756.00
Average annual return		252.00
Average annual return on investment		10.5%

It is the expectation of capital appreciation that attracts institutions and individuals to invest in businesses rather than governments. To justify these expectations a company must develop long-term strategies, that will increase earnings and drive up share prices. This chapter explores why you need a business plan, how to prepare it and the ways in which investment in products, markets, customers, and staff help to increase profits and share prices in the medium-term.

Joe Rich managed a small company. He was paid a basic salary of £25,000. He was also awarded 20 per cent of any surplus of profit after tax over £50,000. This incentive was designed to encourage Joe to increase profits each year. In recent years the profits have grown significantly. However, Joe resigned about three months ago. At about the same time demand for the company product nosedived. It is currently believed that the company will be lucky to break even in the current year. The company employed Vetters Consultants to recruit a new chief executive. When Vetters were being briefed by the Chairman, the remuneration package was one of the major discussion points. The Chairman pointed out that the profit outlook was dismal and that a profit share arrangement was unlikely to attract a suitable recruit. Vetters proposed that a short investigation into the causes of the profit collapse be carried out before the remuneration package was finalised. The Chairman agreed and the investigation ensued.

The following is the report from Vetters Consultants:

                                                    Vetters Consultants
                                                    Dublin 2

The Chairman
Brakes On Ltd
Brentford

Dear Chairman,

We carried out a short investigation into the reasons for the collapse in profits that is currently being experienced by Brakes On Ltd. In our view, the former managing director applied a strategy designed to maximise short-term profits at the expense of future prospects. In order to implement his strategy, it appears to us that Joe Rich did everything in his power to avoid any expenditure that would not result in increased profits in the year when costs were incurred. A number of things helped us to this conclusion.

1. **There was a total freeze on capital expenditure.** As a result, the company fell severely behind in the technology race. In our view any company that wishes to keep pace with competitors should be spending at least 1.5 times the depreciation charge on acquiring new fixed assets. Of course this guideline should not be followed indiscriminately. It is quite acceptable for the spending to fall below this guideline in some years provided that it exceeds it in other years. In this way the expenditure should meet the target over a five-year period. By freezing capital expenditure, the company succeeded in avoiding additional depreciation charges and interest on money borrowed to finance the developments. Such a strategy will certainly work for a couple of years, but failure to keep abreast of the technology race will come back to haunt any business in the way that Brakes On Ltd is currently being affected.

2. **There has been very little effort to recruit new customers.** In our experience, any business can expect to lose at least 25 per cent of customers in a five-year period. This rate of customer attrition was experienced by Brakes On Ltd during the reign of the former managing director. Failure to recruit new customers creeps up on you too gently to notice when you examine monthly or quarterly trends. This strategy was undoubtedly adopted because, in the short-term, one tends to spend far more on the effort to attract new customers than the benefit that is obtained by way of profitable sales.

3. **Virtually no money has been spent on new product development.** In the same way that one tends to lose customers over time the products slowly become outdated and demand falls away as the peak of the product life cycle is passed. Any good company will spend a lot of money on new product development in order to keep pace with changing technology and customer taste. In your industry, the best businesses tend to spend about 4 per cent of turnover on new product development (NPD). During the Joe Rich reign spending on NPD was negligible. This was the most inexcusable offence of all. It has come home to roost in the current year, and whoever is appointed to run the company, will have to make a very large investment to catch up with the new products being offered by competitors.

4. **Staff development has been totally neglected.** In a business such as yours, new thinking and techniques are frequently obtained through effective networking. As far as we can gather, little or no money has been spent on courses, conferences or seminars. Without the injections of enthusiasm that these provide, staff can become jaded, stuck on a treadmill and oblivious to opportunities that are passing before their eyes.

There are two characteristics that link all these failures to keep pace with the evolving business world. Firstly, each type of spending is discretionary. By this I mean that no obvious penalties will be incurred as a result of the failure to invest in the way that if you don't pay your electricity bill your power supply might be cut off. Secondly, the financial results will be bolstered in the short-term by not spending but the longer term consequences can be devastating. To put this into perspective, the returns from development expenditure do not usually provide an immediate payback.

Returns from Development Expenditure

	Payout	Return
Capital investment	Now	2 to 5 years
Customer development	Now	1 to 5 years
Product development	Now	2 to 5 years
Staff development	Now	1 to 20 years

I am sorry that this report paints a distressing picture of the last three years. I am sure that the worst feature of all is the fact that you will need to approve major 'catch up' expenditure if the business is to survive and thrive.
Yours sincerely,
Vetters Consultants

Health is the greatest blessing that can be conferred on a person or a business. The prudent person will arrange a variety of insurance policies in order to protect their health. These include:

- a sensible diet;
- physical fitness;
- restricted intake of drugs;
- conventional health insurance.

The discretionary expenditures (to develop a business) outlined in the Vetters report are the insurance policies that a sensible business will arrange. Failure to invest in them is a bit like smoking. The effect is not obvious but gradual. Business development expenditure must be invested wisely. Indiscriminate throwing of money at these health insurance policies is even worse than failure to invest. An organisation must carefully evaluate the technologies, products, markets, customers and staff that need to be cultivated. There are some very practical benchmarks. For example:

(a) the 1.5 multiple of capital expenditure to depreciation suggested by Vetters. This multiple crosses industry boundaries better than some of the other benchmarks;

(b) in the pharmaceutical industry it is widely acknowledged that you must spend up to 15 per cent of sales revenue on new product development. Of course, this level of NPD expenditure would be excessive in more stable industries. The wise organisation will find out and spend at least the industry norm;

(c) research has revealed that it costs five times as much to recruit a new customer as it does to retain an existing customer. This points to the need to treat existing customers with tender loving care. However, it is inevitable that some customers will be lost. To combat this the organisation must invest in marketing designed to woo new customers;

(d) the wise organisation will commit at least 4 per cent of payroll expenditure to staff development. This guideline does not differ significantly from industry to industry. The trouble is that the payback is difficult to monitor. When an employee learns and uses a new technique, it is hard to calculate the improvement in profits that results.

The Five-Year Planning Horizon

Earlier in the book I stressed the importance of preparing a budget and of comparing actual performance against it. Further planning is required to develop the business. You need a five-year business plan. It need not be done in the same detail as the budget. For example, it is unlikely that you will be able to predict the volumes that you will sell or the customers that will buy them. Table 11.1 shows how the business plan should be prepared and presented.

Table 11.1: Brakes on Ltd – Five year Business Plan and Shareholder Value Analysis

	Current	Year 1	Year 2	Year 3	Year 4	Year 5
Sales	546429	765000	880000	1011000	1163000	1338000
Cost of sales	355179	478125	550000	631875	726875	836250
Gross profit	191250	286875	330000	379125	436125	501750
Overhead	-152895	-160650	-184800	-212310	-244230	-280980
Product development	0	-30600	-35200	-40440	-46520	-53520
Market development	0	-45900	-52800	-60660	-69780	-80280
Staff development	-245	-10098	-11616	-13345	-15352	-17662
PBIT	38110	39627	45584	52370	60243	69308
Interest	-1347	-3468	-3756	-4055	-4398	-4774
PBT	36763	36159	41828	48315	55845	64534
Corporation tax	12132	11932	13803	15944	18429	21296
Profit after tax	24631	24227	28025	32371	37416	43238
Dividend	10000	11500	13225	15209	17490	20114
Retained	14631	12727	14800	17162	19926	23124
Asset replacement	0	-5750	-6613	-7604	-8745	-10057
Working capital	-13011	-32786	-17250	-19650	-22800	-26250
Discretionary cash	1620	-25809	-9063	-10092	-11619	-13183
Payroll	180322	252450	290400	333630	383790	441540
Depreciation	10000	11500	13225	15209	17490	20114

[1] Sales growth 40 per cent in year one 15 per cent p.a. thereafter.
[2] Gross margin to increase to 37.5 per cent of sales.
[3] Operating costs to be reduced through a cost reduction programme to 21 per cent sales
[4] Development expenditure: (a) products 4 per cent of sales, (b) markets 6 per cent of sales and (c) staff 4 per cent of salaries and wages.
[5] Taxation 33 per cent of profit before tax. This reflects the fact that the taxable profit will be higher than the operating profit.
[6] Technology provision 1.5 times depreciation charge.
[7] Stock 7 per cent of sales. Trade debtors 18 per cent of sales. Trade creditors 10 per cent of sales.
[8] Dividend growth at 15 per cent p.a..
[9] Interest at 10 per cent p.a. on net bank borrowings.

In spite of the pre-tax profit of £36,763, Brakes On Ltd was in severe financial difficulties. Sales had nosedived and overhead costs were far too high. At the core of the new business plan were proposals to raise sales by 40 per cent and to reduce overheads from 28 per cent to 21 per cent of sales.

Shareholder value analysis is based on converting the forecast profit and loss accounts into a discretionary cash format. It is designed to establish whether a draft business plan is creating or destroying value. Special features are:

(a) the highlighting of development costs as separate items;

(b) a deduction to reflect the proposed spending on fixed assets in excess of the depreciation charge;

(c) a deduction to reflect the cash that will be invested in stocks and trade debtors as sales grow;

(d) an addition to reflect the impact of additional supplier credit on the cash balance.

The key factor in the shareholder value analysis is the fact that in each year the net cash flow will not be sufficient to service the business plan. Increasing bank borrowings and a trend towards overtrading are the consequences. The business plan will destroy some of the shareholder value. It is interesting to note that the ROI in the proposed business plan is 15.9 per cent, and yet shareholder value is being destroyed.

The board suggested two modifications to the business plan that they believed could be achieved. The revised shareholder value analysis is shown in Table 11.2.

Table 11.2: Brakes On Ltd – Revised Business Plan

	Current	Year 1	Year 2	Year 3	Year 4	Year 5
Sales	546429	765000	880000	1011000	1163000	1338000
Cost of sales	355179	478125	550000	631875	726875	836250
Gross profit	191250	286875	330000	379125	436125	501750
Overhead [1]	-152895	-156825	-176000	-197145	-220970	-247530
Product development	0	-30600	-35200	-40440	-46520	-53520
Market development	0	-45900	-52800	-60660	-69780	-80280
Staff development	-245	-10098	-11616	-13345	-15352	-17662
PBIT	38110	43452	54384	67535	83503	102758
Interest	-1347	-493	662	2490	5170	8953
Profit before tax	36763	42959	55046	70025	88673	111711
Corporation tax	12132	14176	18165	23108	29262	36865
Profit after tax	24631	28783	36881	46917	59411	74846
Dividend	10000	11500	13225	15209	17490	20114
Retained	14631	17283	23656	31708	41921	54732
Asset replacement	0	-5750	-6613	-7604	-8745	-10057
Working capital [2]	-13011	-9836	-13800	-15720	-18240	-21000
Discretionary cash	1620	1697	3243	8384	14936	23675
Payroll	180322	252450	290400	333630	383790	441540
Depreciation	10000	11500	13225	15209	17490	20114

[1] Overheads to be reduced by 0.5 per cent of sales in each year.
[2] Debtors were to be reduced to 15 per cent of additional sales in each year.

The revised plan is very attractive because:

(a) the return on investment will be 21 per cent in year 5;

(b) the business will have generated £94,532 of surplus cash. This can be used to increase the dividend or to invest more heavily in discretionary development;

(c) if the discretionary cash is not used for dividends the shareholders' funds will more than double from £125,411 to £294,711;

(d) the discretionary cash is worth £1.73 per share. We must discount this at 12 per cent (the return expected by shareholders) using the net present value technique outlined in Chapter 9. This gives an NPV of £1.10 per share. The workings are as shown in Tables 11.3, 11.4 and 11.5.

Table 11.3: Shareholder Value – Breaks On Ltd

	Year 1	Year 2	Year 3	Year 4	Year 5
Discretionary cash	1,697	3,243	8,384	14,936	23,675
Discount factor 12 %	0.893	0.797	0.712	0.636	0.567
NPV	1,515	2,585	5,969	9,499	13,424
Shares in issue	30,000	30,000	30,000	30,000	30,000
Share value added	5.1p	8.6p	19.9p	31.7p	44.7p

Table 11.4: Balance Sheets – Brakes On Ltd

	Current	Year 1	Year 2	Year 3	Year 4	Year 5
Plant cost	100000	115000	132250	152088	174901	201136
Depreciation	22000	33500	46725	61934	79423	99538
Book value	78000	81500	85525	90154	95478	101598
Stock	38250	53550	61600	70770	81410	93660
Debtors	98357	114750	132000	151650	174450	200700
Cash	17579	20070	26615	39901	61694	94532
	232186	269870	305740	352475	413032	490490
Share capital	30000	30000	30000	30000	30000	30000
Reserves	95411	112694	136350	168058	209979	264711
Term loan	30000	25000	20000	15000	10000	5000
Creditors	54643	76500	88000	101100	116300	133800
Tax	12132	14176	18165	23108	29262	36865
Dividend	10000	11500	13225	15209	17490	20114
	232186	269870	305740	352475	413032	490490

The most important feature of these balance sheets is the large cash balance. This provides the capacity for substantial extra strategic expenditure.

Table 11.5: Cash Flow Statements – Brakes On Ltd

	Current	Year 1	Year 2	Year 3	Year 4	Year 5
PBIT	38110	43452	54384	67535	83503	102758
Depreciation	10000	11500	13225	15209	17490	20114
Interest	-1347	-493	662	2490	5170	8953
Dividends paid	-8696	-10000	-11500	-13225	-15209	-17490
Taxation	-9453	-12132	-14176	-18165	-23108	-29262
Term loan	-5000	-5000	-5000	-5000	-5000	-5000
Free cash flow	23614	27327	37595	48844	62846	80073
Stock	-6072	-15300	-8050	-9170	-10640	-12250
Debtors	-15613	-16393	-17250	-19650	-22800	-26250
Creditors	8674	21857	11500	13100	15200	17500
Investment	0	-15000	-17250	-19838	-22813	-26235
Change for year	10603	2491	6545	13286	21793	32838
Opening cash	6976	17579	20070	26615	39901	61694
Closing cash	17579	20070	26615	39901	61694	94532

The most interesting feature in these statements is the strong cash flow in year 1. The reduction in debtors from 18 per cent to 15 per cent meant that only £16,393 was to be invested in debtors in year 1 in spite of the 40 per cent growth in sales. Strategic cash flow will be further discussed in Chapter 12.

Overall the revised business plan is attractive. Remember that it requires:

(a) consistent reduction in overheads. These will become progressively more difficult to achieve as savings are sought from an increasingly efficient base;

(b) reduction in debtors' days from 65.7 to 54.8. This will also be a tall order.

YOUR BUSINESS PLAN AND SHAREHOLDER VALUE

The crucial issue of this chapter is that you need a business plan that will create enhanced shareholder value. There are six steps in this process.

1. Predict the sales in each of the five years.

2. Estimate the operating costs including cost reduction initiatives.

3. Calculate the development expenditure. Percentages of sales, as used in Brakes On Ltd, simplify this task.

4. Work out the average net bank borrowings through the years and apply

the expected interest rate.

5. Compute the additional fixed and working capital investment as sales grow.

6. Estimate the corporation tax bill based on the predicted profits.

7. Prepare shareholder value analyses, balance sheets and cash flow statements.

Using a spreadsheet helps to simplify calculations that will be used in each of the five years. The computations for Brakes On Ltd were done on a spreadsheet. This model should help you to construct a business plan that is both attractive and attainable.

SUMMARY

To make a business investment attractive, it is necessary to promise the prospect of capital appreciation. Without this, investors would be well advised to stick to government stocks. Apart from takeover speculation, the only thing that will drive share prices upwards is the promise of increasing profits. The extra profits can only come from a well-conceived business plan. The core aspects of such a plan are:

- new products;
- new markets;
- new customers;
- new technology.

Investment in these areas has two major characteristics: it will increase cost, and thus decrease profits in the short term and it is optional. Failure to invest in business development rarely results in a rapid decline in profits. The decline creeps up on the business as customers are lost to more forward looking competitors. The temptation to neglect development expenditure is seductive. The management of any business that offers profit based bonuses to senior executives can be tempted to sacrifice long-term prospects for short-term bonuses. Three things are required if a business is to resist this temptation.

1. A good five-year business plan.

2. A board attuned to seeking enhanced shareholder value.

3. A staff attuned to seeking new products, markets, customers and technology.

CHAPTER 12

STRATEGIC CASH FLOW ANALYSIS: MINDING YOUR CORPORATE HEART

The heart is probably your most vital organ. If it stops pumping blood, you die. Similarly if a business runs out of cash, it dies. In previous chapters I have argued that your company needs a detailed budget and a five-year business plan. When your profit plan has been developed it is essential to ensure that you will have enough cash to finance it. There are eight cash pressure points as a business develops.

1. Payment of interest and tax.

2. Obligations to repay loans and interest.

3. Increased investment in stocks and debtors as a result of inflation.

4. Payment of dividends.

5. Increased investment in stocks and debtors as a result of growth.

6. Replacement of worn out fixed assets.

7. Extra fixed assets to support growth in output.

8. Investment in other businesses. This can be by taking a strategic minority stake or by takeover.

You must pay the first three items on the list. The others are discretionary. You can even choose not to grow and adopt a pricing policy that facilitates such a strategy.
    Where will the cash come from? There are eight major sources.

1. Cash left over from the previous accounting period.

2. Gross operating cash flow for the period = operating profit plus depreciation.

3. Increased supplier credit as a result of inflation.

4. Increased supplier credit as a result of growth.

5. Proceeds from the disposal of assets and businesses.

6. Loan receipts.

7. Proceeds from the issue of additional shares.

8. Capital grants.

Figure 12.1: Blood Flowing Through the Business

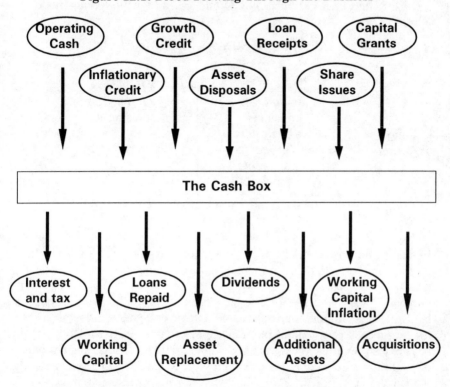

If the cash available from the eight major sources is less than the total of the eight demands, then the plan cannot be funded (see Figure 12.1). It will be necessary to restrict development initiatives. The principal target of the spending reduction is usually investments. They are interesting rather than essential. If postponement or cancellation still leaves insufficient funds to pay for the plan, you should consider postponing all or part of the capital investment programme. This is not an attractive option as tired old assets tend to break down frequently, prove costly to repair and portray an image of a shoddy organisation. Nevertheless, if funds will not be available to pay for replacements, a business should accept that postponement is preferable to excessive debt.

In planning for business development, the first step is to predict the funds that you will have available. For this purpose it is wise to deduct the interest, tax, loan repayments and dividends from the cash flow from operating activities. What remains is called the free cash flow It will be available to develop your business. Furthermore, pressure on cash can be eased by reduction in working capital (lower stocks or debtors and extra supplier credit). Equally, pressure on cash can be increased by extra working capital (longer stockholding or customer credit or reduced supplier credit). The strategic cash flows in a business plan can be summarised in the following model.

Figure 12.2: Strategic Cash Model

	Transfusions	**Extrusions**
Long Term	Opening cash Share issues Free cash flow Loan proceeds Capital Grants Asset disposals	Fixed assets Acquisitions
Short Term	Working capital	Working capital

In this model, cash flows are divided into long-term and short-term components. Long-term transfusions should at least equal long-term extrusions. Otherwise the business is borrowing short-term funds to pay for long-term purposes. This is a recipe for disaster as short-term funds can be withdrawn by the lenders. Another imperative for strategic cash management is that the long-term sources should be put in place before they are used. Failure to do so is like committing yourself to buy a house without first having a promise of a mortgage. Avonmore Foods plc provides a classic example of correctly funded strategic growth. The cash flow statement is presented in the format of the FRSSE.

Table 12.1: Avonmore Foods plc: Cash Flow Statements

£'000	1991	1991	1992	1992
Operating cash flow [(1)]		29,479		31,253
Cash from other sources				
Interest received	1,363		1,727	
Tax recovered	976		—	
Sale of assets	926		1,485	
Loans received	21,428		—	
Capital grants	6,102		2,306	
Proceeds of share issues	30,522		75	
		61,317		5,593
Applications of cash				
Interest paid	12,009		13,833	
Dividends paid	2,165		4,063	
Corporation tax	—		1,495	
Loans repaid	1,061		4,656	
Capital investment	20,054		22,755	
Acquisitions	5,268		38,652	
		(40,557)		(85,454)
		50,239		(48,608)
Opening cash		12,061		62,300
Closing cash		62,300		13,692
[(1)] Operating profit		26,714		36,509
Depreciation		10,999		13,019
Profit on asset sales		(310)		(65)
Working capital		(7,924)		(18,210)
		29,479		31,253

In 1992, Avonmore used £48.608 million of the cash that had been raised in 1991. Without these funds strategic investment would have had to be severely restricted. The cash flows for 1991, that paved the way for the 1992 expansion, were as follows.

Figure 12.3: Avonmore Cash Management 1991

	Transfusions		Extrusions	
Long Term	Opening cash	12,061	Assets	20,054
	Equity	30,522	Acquisitions	5,268
	Free cash flow	24,507		25,322
	Loans received	21,428		
	Capital grants	6,102		
	Asset disposals	926		
		95,546		
Short Term	Stocks	368	Debtors	6,237
			Creditors	2,055
				8,292
		95,914		33,614

£62.3 million cash available for 1992

Long-term funding totalled £95.546 million and long-term investment totalled £25.322 million. This is a perfect example of how to follow the rules for strategic cash flow. The matrix for 1992 was as follows.

Figure 12.4: Avonmore Cash Management 1992

	Transfusions		Extrusions	
Long Term	Opening cash	62,300	Assets	22,755
	Equity	75	Acquisitions	38,652
	Free cash flow	27,143		61,407
	Capital grants	2,306		
	Asset disposals	1,485		
		93,309		
Short Term	Stocks	5,936	Debtors	16,724
			Creditors	7,422
				24,146
		99,245		85,553

£13.692 million cash available for 1993

Long-term funding totalled £93.309 million and long-term investment totalled £61.407 million. The development plan could not have been financed without the major cash injection in 1991.

In Chapter 11 we examined the business plan of Brakes On Ltd. The first draft showed creation of minimal shareholder value. The cash flow statement is reproduced in Table 12.2 in a strategic format.

Table 12.2: Cash Flow Statement for Brakes On Ltd

	Current	Year 1	Year 2	Year 3	Year 4	Year 5
Opening cash	6,976	17,579	-9,680	-17,558	-25,552	-33,981
Free cash flow	23,614	20,527	26,622	31,494	37,184	43,729
Funds available	30,590	38,106	16,942	13,936	11,632	9,748
Stock	-6,072	-15,300	-8,050	-9,170	-10,640	-12,250
Debtors	-15,613	-39,343	-20,700	-23,580	-27,360	-31,500
Creditors	8,674	21,857	11,500	13,100	15,200	17,500
Investment	0	-15,000	-17,250	-19,838	-22,813	-26,235
Closing cash	17,579	-9,680	-17,558	-25,552	-33,981	-42,737

In the current year, the cash flow is positive due to the freeze on capital investment. This saved Brakes On Ltd from a negative cash position. In all the following years, we see the need for bank loans growing as the investment needs exceed the funds available. The strategic plan is cash negative, and will drive Brakes On Ltd into an overtrading crisis. To solve the problem, Brakes On Ltd must select at least one of the following options and make it work.

1. Reduce the level of investment. This would be a sad solution.

2. Introduce more capital.

3. Increase retained earnings through improved product mix or cost reduction.

4. Arrange additional bank loans.

5. Make or buy stock closer to point of sale.

6. Shorten the average customer credit period.

7. Lengthen the supplier credit period.

As we saw in Chapter 11, the company decided to start a cost reduction programme and to reduce the customer credit period. The second draft (Table 12.3) shows the position being stabilised.

Table 12.3: Second Draft of Cash Flow Statement for Brakes On Ltd

	Current	Year 1	Year 2	Year 3	Year 4	Year 5
Opening cash	6,976	17,579	20,070	26,615	39,901	61,694
Free cash flow	23,614	27,327	37,595	48,844	62,846	80,073
Funds available	30,590	44,906	57,665	75,459	102,747	141,767
Stock	-6,072	-15,300	-8,050	-9,170	-10,640	-12,250
Debtors	-15,613	-16,393	-17,250	-19,650	-22,800	-26,250
Creditors	8,674	21,857	11,500	13,100	15,200	17,500
Investment	0	-15,000	-17,250	-19,838	-22,813	-26,235
Closing cash	17,579	20,070	26,615	39,901	61,694	94,532

In this revised version, we see the major impact from reducing the debtors from 18 per cent to 15 per cent of sales and the benefit to the free cash flow from planned cost reduction. Brakes On Ltd will have a much nicer problem to address if this draft proves to be attainable. The issue will now be whether to spend more cash on business development or to increase the dividends.

Sources of Business Development Funds

The first step in preparing your development plan is to predict how much strategic cash will be available. The major sources for private companies are:

- free cash flow;
- bank loans;
- additional supplier credit;
- capital grants.

Companies quoted on the stock market have an enormous advantage in strategic cash generation. They can raise further capital through the sale of shares. This is called a rights issue. Existing shareholders are given the right to buy new shares in proportion to their current holdings. The vendor in a rights issue usually arranges for it to be underwritten. This means that a friendly institution will buy any shares not purchased by the right-holders. The only practical restriction on using rights issues is that stock market professionals do not like a company to go to this well too often. Share issues are not a real funding possibility for many private companies. The owners simply do not have the cash to subscribe and are not prepared to dilute their shareholdings by selling shares to other potential subscribers. To sell a stake in your company to a venture capital organisation is a possible solution. Sadly, many proprietors tend to close their minds to this type of finance. In my opinion to own 75 per cent of a thriving business is far more attractive than to own 100 per cent of a struggling one.

SUMMARY

Success in business is frequently judged to be the ability to expand and diversify. Cash is the blood that flows through the veins of a business. It finances growth. A problem arises if the transfusions are not sufficient to pay for the increase in assets as a business grows. This is a key reason why a business plan is so important. The sources of cash to fund a business plan must be carefully computed. Frequently, further share capital is not available. This limits the sources of funds to:

- the starting cash;

- the free cash flow;

- proceeds from bank loans, which are constrained by gearing;

- increased credit from suppliers,which is limited by settlement period;

- capital grants;

- proceeds from sale of assets;

- cash released by improved stock turnover and credit control.

The first step is to predict the funds available from these sources. When this has been done the wise business will restrict its development plans to meet the funds available. If the funds are inadequate the business may fail as the corporate heart is not pumping enough cash.

CHAPTER 13

RESISTING UNWANTED TAKEOVER BIDS: INOCULATION

Predators are lurking. They may wish to take over your successful business. Some takeover candidates are happy to accept an offer, if the price is right. For example, the third generation in a family business frequently wish to unlock the cash tied up in their shares. They are not prepared to contribute body, soul and funds to developing the business as their parents and grand-parents did. The last thing that a lot of other owners want is to have to spend a lot of time and money resisting an unwanted bid. They need to develop the weapons that will help them to ward off an unwanted suitor. This chapter is included to help them resist an offer or to drive up the price to an acceptable level. The techniques are similar to the inoculations that are used to protect people against diseases.

Typhoid is a very serious disease. If you visit countries that are exposed to this disease your doctor will advise you to have a typhoid injection before you travel. This should help to build up your resistance to this dreadful dis-ease. In the same way a good financial doctor should be able to provide you with inoculation against an unwanted takeover offer. The key to inoculation is to know what your business is worth. As we will see this involves placing a value on past, present and future profitability.

Tom Keep has been in business for eighteen years. He started 'his' company, Target Ltd, in a small rented premises. The company progressed dramati-cally. In the last financial year, the balance sheet showed net assets of £1.3 million, while the profit and loss account showed a profit after tax of £165,123.

When Tom opened his post the other day, one letter contained a bid from Gobbler plc. It offered to buy Target Ltd for £1.5 million. Since Target had 500,000 shares, the bid was worth £3 per share. Tom's initial reaction was to feel flattered that another company would consider his business to be so valuable. On further consideration Tom decided he would not wish to sell even if he was offered £5 million.

Tom also realised that he would have to discuss the offer with the other shareholders. Over the years Tom had sold shares to a number of parties, to raise the funds that enabled Target Ltd to grow. Forty per cent of the shares were owned by a venture capital company. Another 26 cent were owned by friends and relatives. It occurred to Tom that not all of them might be prepared to refuse the unwanted offer.

Tom sought my advice on how to persuade the other shareholders not to sell the company. I collected the following information.

1. The premises stood in the books at £450,000. Tom believed that if he put them up for sale they would realise close to £1 million.

2. Target had a history of paying small dividends. Last year £20,000 had been paid to shareholders. This was a miserly 12 per cent of the profit after tax. Tom had always argued for small dividends. The venture capital company had supported him. They were interested in capital appreciation, rather than cash income. Many of the other shareholders' were unhappy at the low level of dividends. Their board representative had often argued for higher payments. He had been outvoted by the combination of Tom and the venture capital company. Tom was afraid that some of these shareholders would vote to sell Target as a way of avenging the miserable dividends.

3. Tom had always been prepared to accept a small salary and liberal expenses. Apart from his wish to stay independent, Tom feared that if the company was sold, his ability to pay himself substantial expenses would be curtailed. It was also possible that his low salary would be used as the base upon which increases would be granted.

4. Cost control in the company had not been taken too seriously. Tom wanted all the staff to feel that it was 'a great place to work'. As a result, considerable sums of money were spent in areas that provided questionable returns.

5. Tom believed that the principal reason for the bid was to avail of potential savings (called synergy) that would arise through merging the businesses. The bidder held about 20 per cent and Target about 12 per cent of the 'thingummy' market. Tom pondered the major rationalisation (warehousing, marketing, distribution and administration) that the bidder expected to implement. He expected that many of the Target activities would

be eliminated. He foresaw close downs and redundancies. The expected synergy is a bit like predicting that two plus two will equal five (see Table 13.1).

Table 13.1: Expected Synergy in Gobbler Takeover of Target

£'000	Target	Gobbler	Group
Sales	1,731	2,860	4,591
Cost of sales	1,213	2,022	3,235
Gross profit	518	838	1,356
Overheads	264	499	665
Net profit	254	339	691
Taxation	89	115	235
Profit after tax	165	224	456

The group profit before tax is expected to rise by £98,000 due to savings in overheads. When plans to avail of synergy are being made, three important points should be remembered.

1. The seller should hold out for a fair share of the benefit. The group profit after tax, before allowing for overhead reductions, amounts to £389,000. Target contributes 42.4 per cent to this total. It is reasonable to argue that their contribution to the business combination is 42.4 per cent of the combined profit. This amounts to £193,419. It is to this figure that Target should argue that the price earnings ratio be applied, since the synergy cannot be achieved if the two parties do not merge. Applying this multiple would value the business at £1.93 million.

2. Gobbler Ltd, or any other predator, will be reluctant to share the benefits of the business combination. They will argue that it is their initiative that allows the cost savings to be released.

3. The vast majority of companies that merge, with a view to rationalisation, tend to be disappointed. The savings simply do not come through. It is all very fine to envisage savings on paper. When rationalisation plans are put in place, the savings often prove difficult to achieve. They are sometimes sabotaged by disgruntled staff.

What Should Tom Do?

The key problem for Tom is that he cannot outvote the other shareholders. If Tom had control, he could simply set an unrealistic selling price for Target Ltd, say £25 per share. This would value the business at £12.5 million and should lead to a withdrawal by Gobbler Ltd.

This will probably not work. The other shareholders will outvote Tom. There are two approaches that might work: Tom could make a counter bid, if he could raise the cash, or Tom could try to persuade the other shareholders that the offer is inadequate. This will probably prove difficult because some of them are disgruntled. However, Tom must persuade the other shareholders that prospects for capital appreciation and dividend growth will be more promising if they stay with Target. He will have to prepare and present an attractive and attainable business plan.

The Inoculations

Tom fell into the same trap as many business people. He started to plan his defence too late. The wise manager foresees the danger of a bid long before it arrives. It is then possible to do things to deter an unwanted suitor. For example, it is not wise for any business to carry land and buildings, in the balance sheet, at out of date values. Tom should have got a formal valuation of the £1 million property. He could have included this valuation in the balance sheet.

£'000	Before	After
Land and buildings	450	1,000
Other net assets	850	850
	1,300	1,850
Financed by:		
Share capital	500	500
Revenues reserve	800	800
Revaluation reserve	—	550
	1,300	1,850

This would provide the first plank in his defence. Even disgruntled shareholders would be unlikely to accept a bid of £3 per share when the balance sheet suggests that they are worth £3.70. The value per share is calculated by dividing the net assets by the number of shares in issue.

Bid	Asset value
1,500,000 / 500,000 = £3.00	1,850,000 / 500,000 = £3.70.

The inclusion of an up to date value for property is a practice that I strongly recommend. There are three reasons.

1. It is easier to argue the 'real' value, if the balance sheet includes it.

2. The increased value demonstrates the correct gearing and the level of

security that the assets offer. This is useful when negotiating bank loans.

3. Return on investment (the relationship between profits and assets) is only meaningful when up to date asset valuations are used.

When an unwanted bid is received, it is normal practice for the defenders to promise a dramatic improvement in profits and a greatly increased dividend. This defensive strategy implies that the bid is opportunistic and perfectly timed to capitalise on an expected upsurge. Once again, it is wise to try to pre-empt the hostility by keeping the shareholders sweet. If Target had paid a dividend of £60,000 (36 per cent of the after tax profit) it would probably have achieved this. The promise of a large increase sounds like a late conversion, driven by necessity.

Small companies frequently pay their senior managers low salaries and liberal expenses. If a takeover offer succeeds, these executives can find themselves poorly placed with regard to future emoluments. The new regime may base increases on the low level current emoluments. They may also impose strict limitations on expenses. If Tom had highly supportive shareholders he might have been able to insert a 'poison pill' in company policy. This might trigger a trebling of salary and the automatic signing of a five year service contract as soon a takeover bid succeeded.

In Chapter 10 we examined the need for value for money. If this is not regularly reviewed the potential for making sure that a bid is high enough is limited. The value of a business is partly based on a multiple of the profit after tax (price earnings (PE) ratio). If a business does not consistently seek cost efficiencies, the after tax profit to which the PE multiple is applied will be less than it ought to be. This can lead to an inadequate bid price. Claims for a premium, to compensate for the cost reduction potential, can fall on deaf ears.

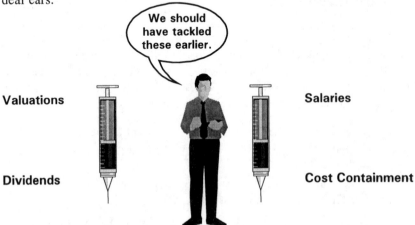

These suggestions should deter the casual bidder or drive up the price.

Important Considerations in a Bid Situation

1. Is the offer in shares, cash or both? The snag about a cash offer is that it will attract capital gains tax. A cash offer will drive up the gearing.

2. Occasionally the buyer company can be seriously overvalued. This can arise through the use of optimistic accounting policies. It can also arise when institutional investors seem to ascribe magical qualities to the chairman or chief executive that are similar to walking on water. In such cases the seller is advised to press for a cash offer. The buyer company will come back down to earth sooner or later.

3. Where the company to be bought is not quoted on a stock market, it is wise to make part of the consideration contingent on future performance. For example, Gobbler Ltd might make an offer in two parts. The first part would be a cash offer of £3 per share. The second part could be ten times the growth in profits, over £164,000, in each of the following three years. A series of payments might result as in Table 13.2.

Table 13.2: Series of Payments following Takeover

Year	Profit after tax	Super profit	Additional payment
1	180,000	16,000	160,000
2	211,000	31,000	310,000
3	235,000	24,000	240,000

Delivery of this growth would add £710,000 to the ultimate price.

4. When buying another business, you must be certain that there are no nasty skeletons in the closet. The prudent buyer will insist on two important conditions. Firstly, a 'due diligence' review must be carried out. This requires that a reporting accountant examine the reliability of the assets and liabilities. For example, the value of stocks or debtors might be overstated or the amount of liabilities understated. Secondly, agreement is needed that the final price will be scaled down by the amount of any valuation errors discovered in the review. For example, Gobbler might offer £1.5 million less any errors uncovered. In a recent case, in which I was the reporting accountant, I discovered that the assets of the pension fund were substantially lower than the expected future obligations. The buyer, quite reasonably, argued that it should reduce the price as it would have to pay a large sum to make the pension fund solvent.

5. A company that is considering an acquisition is well advised to consider the possibility that that business has been 'dressed up' to attract a suitor. For example, if you wished to put a company up for sale, you might put

a freeze on capital expenditure. This would keep the gearing down, and lower the interest and depreciation charges.

Diversification

The go-ahead business is expected to grow and to diversify. Apart from the expectation of increased profits and enhanced shareholder value, it is also true that without diversification you can wind up too dependant on one product or one customer. Growth can be achieved in two ways. The first way, called organic growth, is to expand into new products or new markets. The second way is to buy a business that is in different products or markets. This is called growth by acquisition. It is usually safer to diversify by acquisition than to start from scratch. The main reason for this is that the company you buy has found ways to cope with the special quirks involved in serving its market place. The downside of an acquisition strategy is that the price for a successful business reflects this know-how.

When a company wants to expand there are four possible strategies available to it.

Figure 13.1: The Growth Matrix

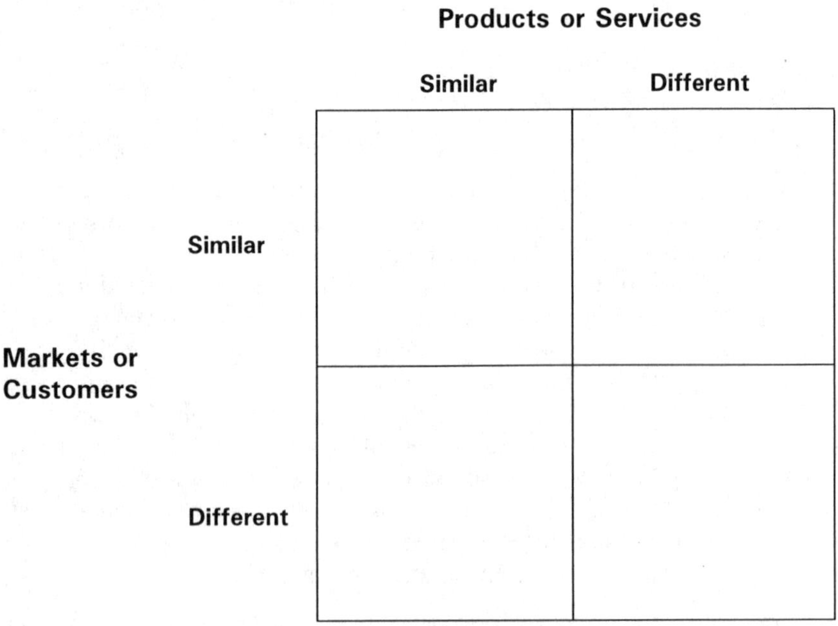

Products or Services

	Similar	Different
Similar		
Different		

Markets or Customers

This matrix shows us the four types of growth. You can:

(a) sell similar products or services to similar customers or in similar markets. This type of expansion is slotted into the top left quadrant of the matrix. It is generally done organically. Knowledge of the products, services, customers and markets makes it the safest of the four approaches;

(b) sell similar products or services to different customers or in different markets. This type of expansion is slotted into the bottom left quadrant of the matrix. It can be done organically or by acquisition. It is more risky. The absence of customer, and/or market knowledge, increases the risk. Nevertheless, product knowledge makes it relatively safe;

(c) sell different products or services to similar customers or in similar markets. This type of expansion is slotted into the top right quadrant of the matrix. It can be done organically or by acquisition. It is more risky. The absence of product knowledge increases the risk. Nevertheless, customer and or market knowledge makes it relatively safe;

(d) sell different products or services to different customers, or in different markets. This type of growth is called conglomerate diversification. It is normally done by acquisition. The absence of knowledge of the products or services, and the customers or markets, make it much more risky. The fact that you do not have either a product or a customer advantage means that you will have to travel down two learning curves, each fraught with dangers, at the same time.

REASONS WHY ONE BUSINESS MIGHT ACQUIRE ANOTHER

1. Acquisition is safer than 'greenfield' development.

2. Combining two businesses offers opportunities for synergy.

3. A good acquisition may provide excellent brands, experienced staff and loyal customers.

4. It is often possible to buy another business for a lower price earnings ratio than your own. The magic is to get the stock market to continue to value the business combination at your PE. For example, Bidder plc wants to buy Seller Ltd. It offers one share for each three Seller shares. If the offer succeeds the share price should rise as shown in Table 13.3.

Table 13.3: Rise in Share Price following Exchange of Shares

	Buyer	**Seller**	**Group**
Shares in issue	10M	3M	11M
Earnings per share	50p	20p	50.9p[1]
PE	15	10	15
Share Price	£7.50	£2.00	£7.64

[1]Combined earnings are £5.6 million.

5.   Under-utilised or undervalued assets.

6.   Access to new products or new markets.

7.   Opportunities to 'unbundle'. This is the polite, modern term for asset stripping. Parts of a diversified business are sold off. The value of the separated parts proves to be higher than that of the previous combination.

Valuation of a Business

The value of a business is composed of two major parts. The first part is based on the total assets minus all of the liabilities. As we saw earlier in this chapter, this part of the valuation can be distorted if assets are incorrectly valued or liabilities are omitted. A buyer can protect itself against these errors by obtaining a warranty relating to the reliability of the balance sheet or arranging that the price be subject to a 'due diligence' examination. The second part of the value is based on the business plan as developed in Chapter 11. The key issue is whether the business is creating or destroying value. A business that is creating value should have three major characteristics. These are:

(a) excellent products;

(b) loyal customers;

(c) high quality staff.

The ongoing value of these characteristics should be computed using the model developed in Chapter 11. As we saw this is done by discounting the cash flows for the next five years. A buyer valuation will be based on the discounted cash flows of the business as a separate entity. A seller valuation will include their contribution to the synergies to be effected. These extremes of value will form the basis for negotiations between the buyer and the seller. The seller valuation is unlikely to be accepted in all cases where asset replacement expenditure must be undertaken or rationalisation costs will be incurred.

SUMMARY

Your company could be a takeover candidate. If you do not have a controlling interest you may not be able to resist a bid. A business with a large spread of shareholders is more likely to fall into the clutches of a predator. If the directors want to avoid a hostile bid they must inoculate themselves by:

- running their business efficiently;

- being generous in paying dividends;

- having a business plan designed to grow profits, reduce risk and enhance shareholder value;

- inserting a 'poison pill';

- keeping the value of appreciating assets up to date.

When a company identifies a takeover candidate, it should discover why it might be for sale. There are three potential snags.

1. The asset base may have been deliberately run down.

2. There may be overvalued assets or understated liabilities.

3. The industry sector may be moving from boom to recession.

The best inoculation against an unwanted takeover bid is growth. This can be achieved organically or by acquisition. Product and market diversification are reasonably safe. Knowledge of the technology or the customers provide the protection. Conglomerate diversification is more risky. The fact that your product and customer experience are limited make it dangerous. If you are considering a conglomerate diversification you are advised to remember two important facts. Firstly, it has gone out of fashion among big businesses. They are more interested in 'unbundling' (separating non-core activities) by sell off or flotation. Secondly, it may seem surprising but the financial priorities in another sector may be significantly different from your base of experience. The wise acquirer will make sure to retain the key staff in any company they buy. This will enable the buyer to capitalise on the product and customer edge that drove a substantial goodwill premium.

GLOSSARY

Accounting Standards Board The body charged with making the rules for recording and reporting complex business transactions.

Accruals Costs that have been incurred but have not been charged to you. Electricity and phone charges are examples. The cost must be charged in the profit and loss account and the liability recognised in the balance sheet.

Acquisition The purchase of another business where control passes to the buyer.

Activity based costing The procedure that enables costs to be collected by type of activity, rather than by type of expenditure so that they can be attributed to products or customers correctly.

Assets The things that a business owns. The assets are collected, valued and reported in the balance sheet.

Balance sheet A picture of a business that shows what it owns (the assets) and how the ownership is financed (through liabilities and shareholders' funds).

Call option The right but not the obligation to purchase a foreign currency at a predetermined price on a future date.

Conglomerate diversification Expansion of a business into an area that requires it to supply a different range of products to a different group of customers.

Current In accounting amounts are classified as current if they will have to be paid or will be realised within one year of the balance sheet date.

Depreciation The process through which the loss of value arising as a long-term asset is used in a business is recognised. The loss must be charged against profits and deducted from the value of the asset.

Direct cost A cost incurred specifically to create a product or service. The raw material used by a manufacturing business is the classic example of a direct cost.

Dividend cover The relationship between the profit attributable to the ordinary shareholders and the amount paid to them. Businesses that are growing rapidly should retain a significant proportion of profits and have a high dividend cover. Businesses that are not growing rapidly will not need to retain a significant proportion of profits and should have a low dividend cover.

Due diligence An investigation carried out after a company buys a business and wants to ensure that the assets have not been overstated or the liabilities understated.

Fixed cost A cost that tends to remain stationary regardless of changes in output. A classic example is rent.

Forward purchase agreement A contract that enables a business to buy a foreign currency at a predetermined price on a future date.

Forward sale agreement A contract that enables a business to sell a foreign currency at a predetermined price on a future date.

Gearing The relationship between the funds provided to a business by its owners and its bankers. The higher the proportion of bank debt in the mix, the more risky the business is.

Indirect cost A cost that is incurred for the general good of a business, rather than to create a specific product or service. The classic example is the salary of the chief executive.

Interest cover The relationship between the profit before interest and the interest cost. The lower the cover the more risky a business is.

Interest rate swop A method for making an interest rate fixed. The swop can occur because a cash rich business wants to protect itself against the risk of a fall in interest rates, whereas a borrower wants to protect itself against a rise in interest rates.

Internal rate of return The maximum interest rate that a business can afford to pay, to borrow funds for capital investment. The cash flowing from the use of the asset is exactly equal to the obligations to repay capital and interest.

Liabilities Amounts owed by a business as reported in its balance sheet. The liabilities are classified in two categories: those due and payable in under one year and those due and payable in beyond one year.

Margin The amount that is left after all the costs have been charged against sales.

Merger The marriage of two businesses of similar size in which neither party can be deemed to have a controlling interest.

Modified internal rate of return An investment appraisal tool that measures the maximum interest rate which a business can afford to pay, and still be able to meet exactly its capital and interest obligations. The cash flows earned from the investment are deemed to earn a specific return that is based on the overall earning power of the business.

Net present value An investment appraisal tool that converts future cash flows into their value at the time of investment.

Payback A capital investment analysis tool that measures how long it will take for the cash returns derived from using the asset to exactly equal the cost of the investment.

PE Ratio A method used to value a business at a multiple of its profit after tax. The more attractive the prospects for a business, the higher will be the PE ratio applied to it.

Poison pill A weapon used to discourage an unwanted takeover bid. For example, a successful bid could trigger a trebling of salaries and the inception of ten-year service contracts for directors.

Prepayments Costs that have been paid for but have not yet provided value to the buyer. The major example is insurance. It is normally paid for one year in advance.

Profitability index A device used to pinpoint the best investments. It is essential to use it when the value of proposals exceeds the amount available to pay for them.

Proposed dividend The amount that the directors set aside for payment to shareholders after approval of the dividend at the annual general meeting.

Put option The right but not the obligation to sell a foreign currency at a predetermined price on a future date.

Return on equity The relationship between the profits earned by a business and the funds that the shareholders have invested in the business.

Return on investment The relationship between the profits earned by a business and the assets that are required in order to earn the profits.

Revenue reserve The aggregate of profits earned on behalf of shareholders that have been retained to contribute towards funding the growth in assets as the business expands.

Segmental analysis The report of the sales, profits and assets broken down so as to explain the performance of different parts of the business. In large businesses, reports are required by product group and by market.

Trade creditors Amounts owed to suppliers that have provided goods but have not yet been paid for them.

Trade debtors Amounts owed to a business by customers who have bought goods but have not yet paid for them.

Variable cost A cost that rises and falls in direct response to changes in volume. The classic example is raw material used by a manufacturer to make a product.

Working capital The investment in stock and debtors less creditors that it is necessary for a business to make in order to support its sales.

Index

ALSO AVAILABLE FROM BLACKHALL PUBLISHING

The Being Successful in...Series

This new series of practical books provides an accessible and user-friendly approach to the common problems encountered by small to medium-sized, growing businesses. The series concentrates on problems encountered during the all-important development phase, when businesses are starting to grow and need to cope with a range of unfamiliar, difficult and often competing issues.

The books in the series are comprehensive yet concise, and treat the topics in question succinctly and without recourse to jargon. Practical examples, checklists and pointers on to further sources of help and advice are included to supplement the text.

Titles Available:

Being Successful in...Customer Care, Veronica Canning, £12.99
1-901657-30-2

Being Successful in...Report Writing, Harris Rosenberg, £12.99
1-901657-19-1

Being Successful in...Patents, Copyright and Trade Marks, Peter Hanna, £12.99
1-901657-28-0

Being Successful in...Budgeting, Evelyn Hempenstall, £9.99,
1-901657-27-2

Being Successful in...Time Management, Tom McConalogue, £9.99
1-901657-20-5

Being Successful in...Presentations, Lynda Byron, £9.99
1-901657-56-6

Available September 1999
Being Successful in...Motivation, Veronica Canning, £9.99
1-901657-31-0

The above books can be purchased at any good bookshop or
direct from:
BLACKHALL PUBLISHING
26 Eustace Street
Dublin 2
Ireland

Telephone: +353 (0)1-677-3242; Fax: +353 (0)1-677-3243;
e-mail: blackhall@tinet.ie